The original Brian Jones Rollin' Stones including "Stu" Ian Stewart at The Marquee Club at the end of 1962. The Stones would return in 1986 to play tribute to "stu" in a surprise concert with Diz and the Doorman as support.

ALL RIGHTS RESERVED. NO PART OF THIS PUBLICATION MAY BE PRODUCED, STORED IN A RETRIEVAL SYSTEM, OR TRANSMITTED IN ANY FORM OR BY ANY MEANS, ELECTRONIC, MECHANICAL, PHOTOCOPYING, RECORDING OR OTHERWISE, WITHOUT PRIOR PERMISSION OF THE COPYRIGHT HOLDERS.
THIS EDITION PUBLISHED IN 1994.
BY VINYL EXPERIENCE LTD, LONDON, ENGLAND.

**THE ROLLING STONES
THE BRIAN JONES STORY
PHOTOGRAPHIC CREDITS**

REX 17, 19, 21, 22, 23, 24, 28, 29, 35, 36, 37, 43, 45, 49, 53, 55, 56, 57, 64, 68, 69, 71.

DEZO HOFFMANN 1, 2, 3, 12, 13 + (Book Cover)

MARK SHARRATT 25, 26, 31.

PIC PRESS 4, 5, 10, 11, 18, 30, 34, 38, 42, 44, 46, 47, 65, 66, 67, (Rear Book Jacket)

TONY GALE 6, 7, 8, 9, 14, 15, 32, 33, 52, 58, 59, 61.

L.F.I. 16, 20, 27, 39, 40, 41, 48, 50, 51, 54, 60, 63, 70, 71.

Thanks to Andrew O'Neil for invaluable information and drinking partner
(No murder stories in this book) just a photographic compliment.
Big hug to Acrelda, Laurie and all of the vinyl experience crew.
Book concept and design by Mark Hayward and Mike Edgar of Printkings.

One of the earliest photo calls at The Marquee Club (Now in Charing Cross Road, London W1).

BRIAN, KEITH, MICK, CHARLIE, BILL and Ian Stewart got together for the general purpose of playing at the Bricklayers' Arms. Over Christmas 1962 (Boxing Day) the ROLLING STONES (as yet un-named) had a booking in the Piccadilly Club. Early in 1963 they deputised for Alexis Korner at the Marquee Club. Following this they had semi regular gigs at the Marquee, Eel Pie Island and the Ealing Club. They recorded at IBC Studios. In February the ROLLING STONES began an eight month residency in Richmond, at the Crawdaddy Club, Station Hotel......

1963

APRIL

28 Andrew Oldham and Eric Easton saw the ROLLING STONES at Richmond and signed a management deal the next day.

MAY

10 First official recording session at Olympic Studios. Andrew Oldham produced, tracks included "Come On", "I Wanna Be Loved".

JUNE

7 "Come On"/"I Wanna Be Loved" released and they appeared on "Thank Your Lucky Stars" - their first television appearance.

13 Received first British national daily newspaper plaudit from Patrick Doncaster of the Daily Mirror, who described the STONES and the scene at the Station Hotel and the "new dance" - "....which you will see nowhere in the world but Richmond.... all you need is a crowded room - the ROLLING STONES' new record 'Come On' .... or maybe you just like to listen to the music which is very exciting anyway".

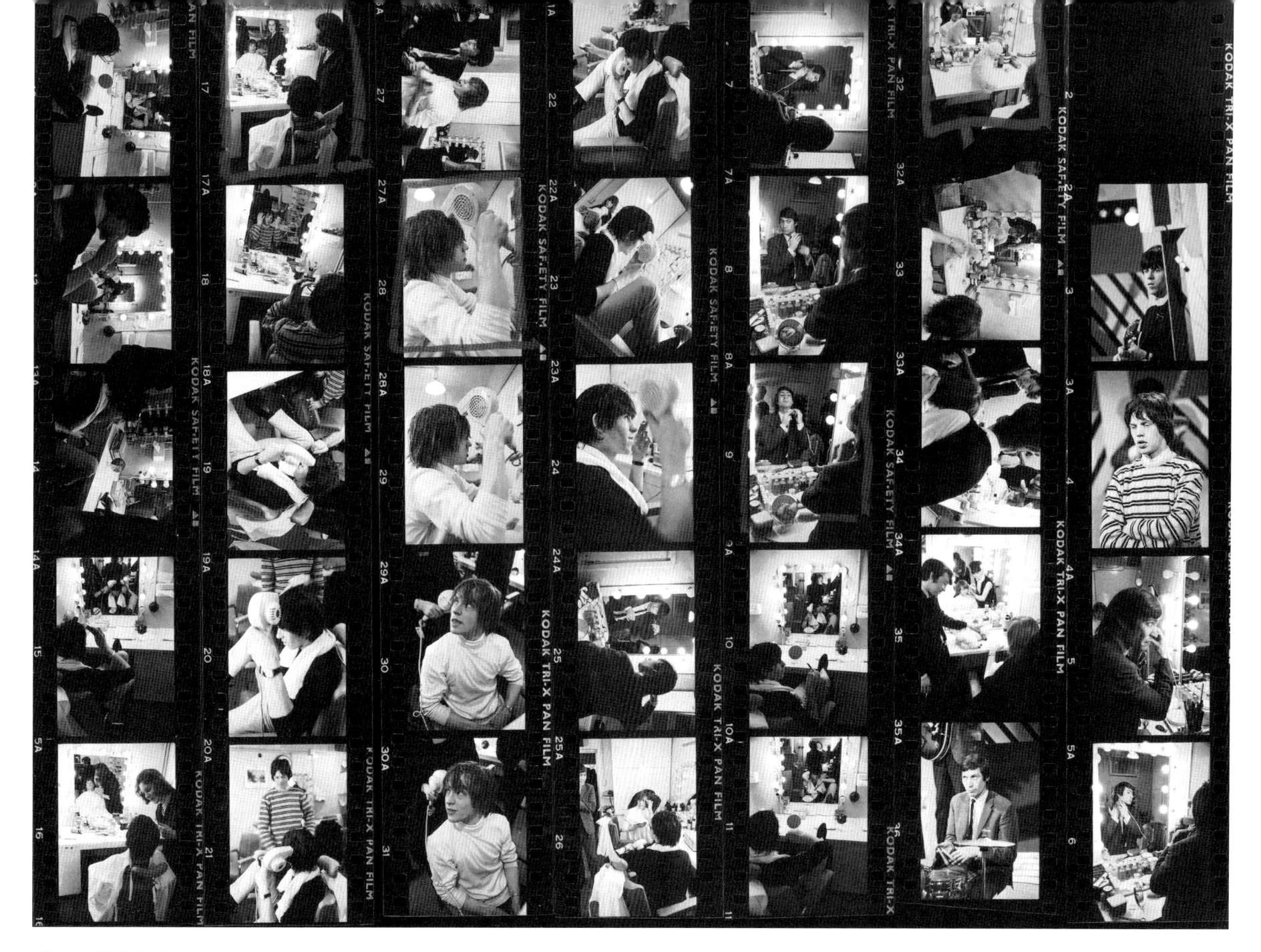

Above - THE STONES mimed to "It's All Over Now" at Alpha TV Studios in Aston Birmingham, promotional videos were virtually unheard of in those days hence the constant appearances on the major TV shows of the day such as this one on "Thank Your Lucky Stars".

SEPTEMBER
29 First English tour with Everley Brothers and Bo Diddley opens at the New Victoria, London, with 30 dates, concluding on November 3.

NOVEMBER
1 Release of "I Wanna Be Your Man"/"Stoned".

1964

JANUARY
6 The ROLLING STONES start tour, topping the bill for the first time, with the Ronnettes.

FEBRUARY
21 Release of "Not Fade Away"/Little by Little".

APRIL
18 ROLLING STONES at Wembley Empire Pool, Mad Mod Ball.

20-21 Stones fly to Montreux for an International TV Festival.

Live at the BBC Radio Playhouse Theatre, Charing Cross Road, London 13/3/64

APRIL

22 Daily Mirror reported: "Mr Wallace Snow-croft, President of the National Federation of Hairdressers offered a free haircut to the next number one group or soloist in the pop chart, adding: 'THE ROLLING STONES are the worst. One of them looks as if he has got a feather duster on his head'".

26 New Musical Express Poll Winners Concert at Wembley.

Release of LP "The Rolling Stones".

MAY

1 Jack Hutton, Editor of Melody Maker, reporting as guest columnist in the Daily Mirror: As if by a pre-arranged signal, all five simultaneously pulled down the skin under their eyes and pushed up their noses. Believe me, it's frightening...."

10 In "The People", Jimmy Saville: "The STONES are a great team for having a laugh and dress very clean and smart when they relax, contrary to what lots of people think...."

A young Phil Spector listens to the first playback of his performance with the maracas on "Little by Little" while Graham Nash (far left) listens in at Regent Sound Studios, London.

MAY Cont'd

11 Paula James, Daily Mirror, reports that MICK JAGGER had undergone a shampoo and set at BBC TV 2 studios, She added, "MICK hasn't got a hairdryer, he just walks about".

27 Daily Mirror: a headmaster ruled that Beatle haircuts were in but ROLLING STONES cuts were out. Eleven boys were suspended from Woodlands Comprehensive School, Coventry, where they wore their hair like MICK JAGGER.

JUNE

3 First American tour opens on June 3, concludes on June 20

23 ROLLING STONES arrive home - riots at airport from the crowds welcoming them back.

26 Release of "It's All Over Now"/"Good Times, Bad Times".

Andrew Loog Oldham along with Brian Mick and Keith, share a drink while Gene Pitney is called in to play piano on Little by Little the sixth track on the STONES first LP. Now I've got a witness The 5th track is dedicated to uncle Gene and Phil (spector) on the Decca LP mono LK 4605.

JULY
8 "It's All Over Now" at Number 1. KEITH, BILL and BRIAN attend the Beatles' party at the Dorchester Hotel to celebrate the premiere of "A Hard Day's Night".

24 ROLLING STONES appear at Blackpool and flee from stage when a teenage mob riot at the Empress Ballroom.

AUGUST
3 Third Pop Concert held at the Marquess of Bath's home, Longleat House, ROLLING STONES HEADLINE - 200 faint.

7 ROLLING STONES back at Richmond for Jazz and Blues Festival (see photo on page 16).

8 Concert at The Hague - audience got out of hand and two girls had their clothes ripped off in the audience.

10 Manchester, Bellevue, New Elizabethan Ballroom, two policemen faint, more than 50 policemen needed to control audience.

13 Douglas Ballroom, Isle of Man - 7000 in audience.

18 Quick tour to the Channel Islands.

SEPTEMBER
5 British tour .... with Charlie and Inez Foxx, until October 11.

In the Melody Maker awards THE STONES are voted Britain's Most Popular Rock Group and also accolade for the Best Song, "Not Fade Away".

OCTOBER
20 Paris Olympia - first show in Paris .... hundreds of stampeding fans broke windows at the theatre after the show. The police were called - riots in the streets, shop windows broken etc. 150 arrests, £1400 damage at Olympia.

23 Fly to United States for 12 dates, including the Academy of Music and the Ed Sullivan Show.

NOVEMBER
13 Release of "Little Red Rooster"/"Off the Hook".

DECEMBER
21 Publication of pocket book "Ode to a High Flying Bird" by Charlie Watts (written in 1961, the story of Charlie 'Bird' Parker). Republished by myself in 1991 on UFO jazz label.

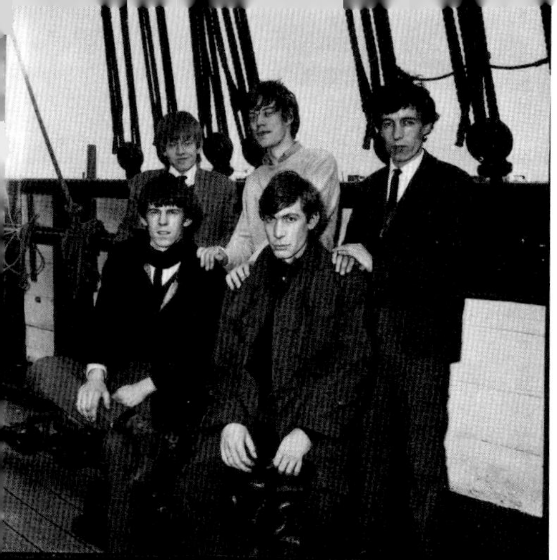

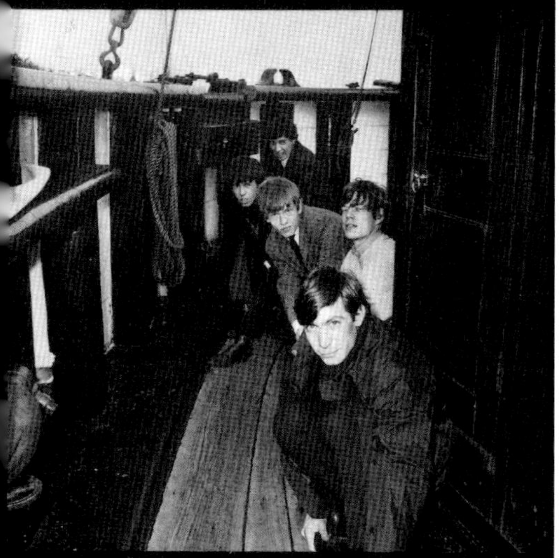

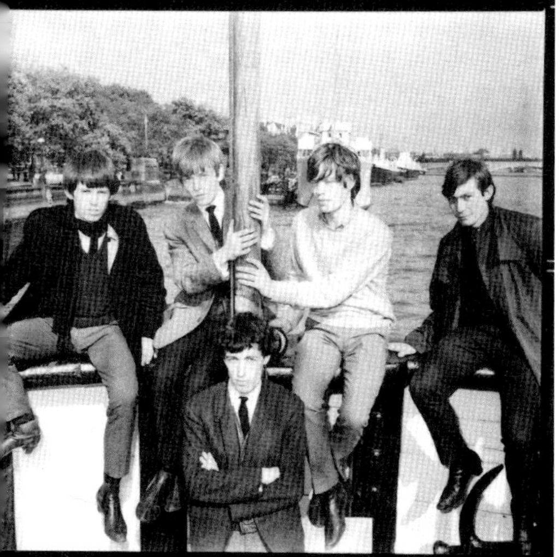

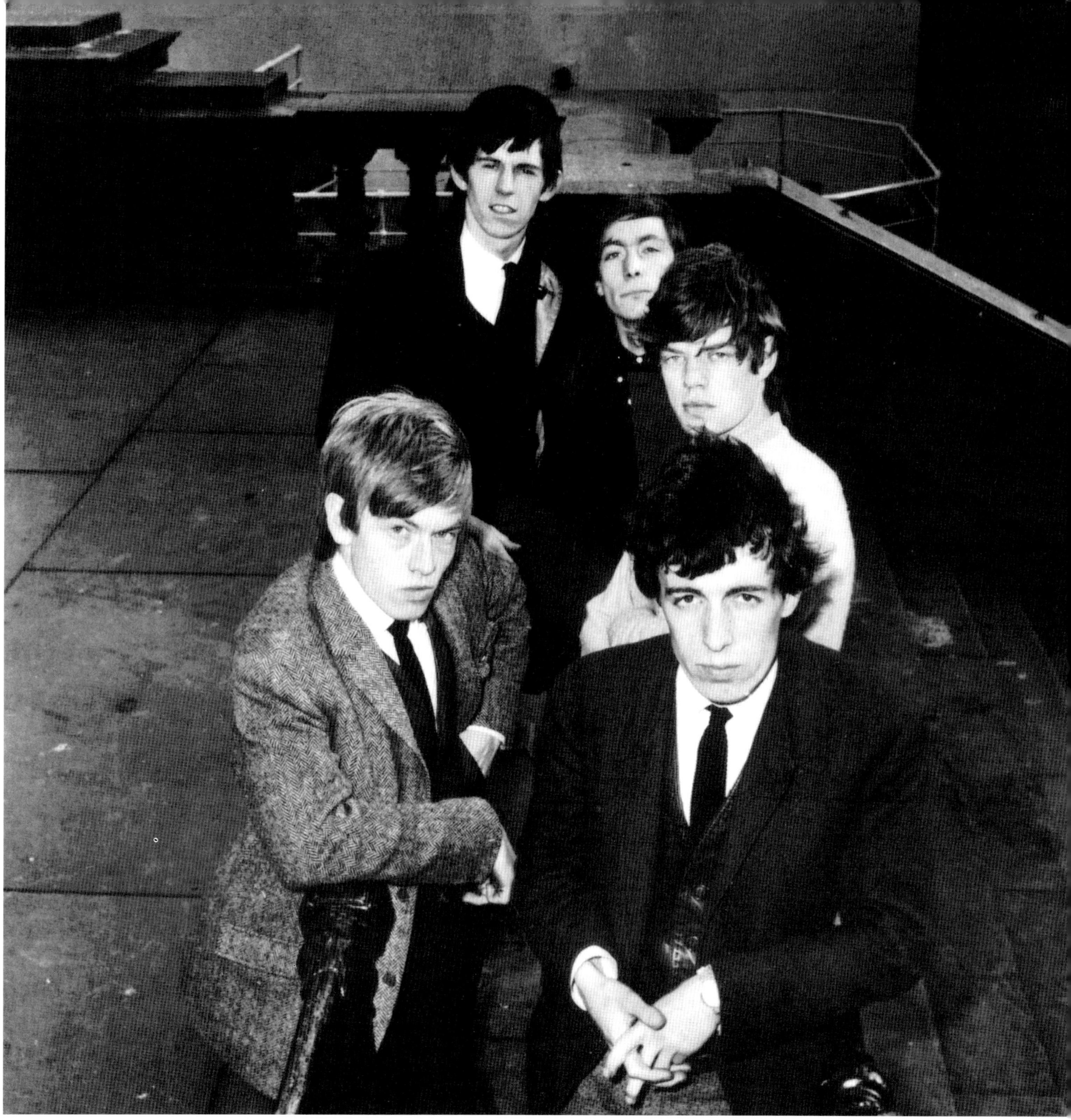

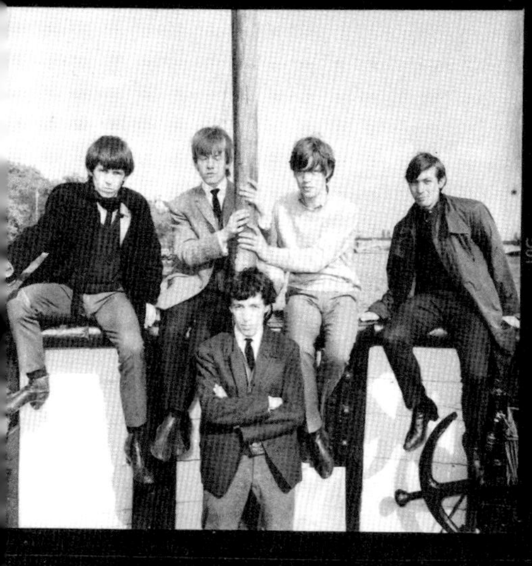

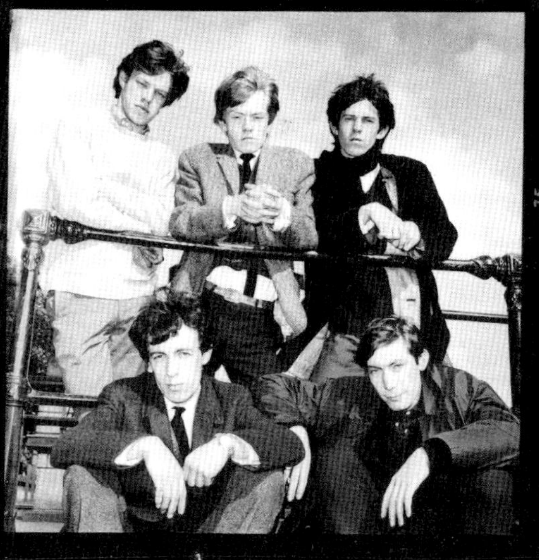

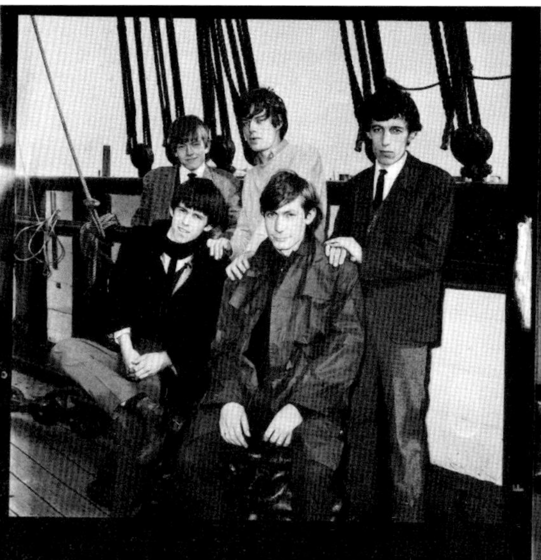

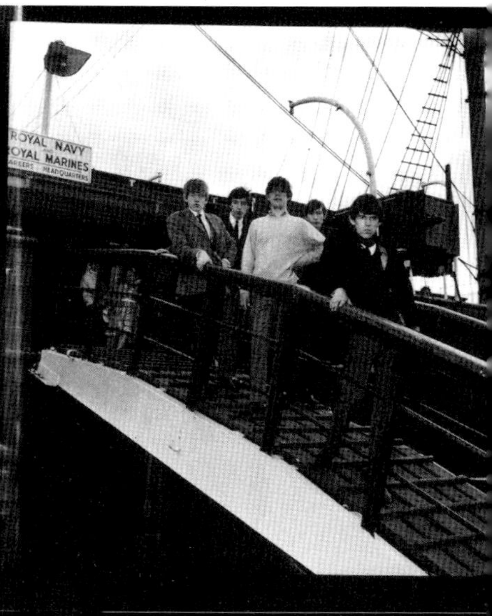
ROYAL NAVY
ROYAL MARINES

HMS Discovery, discovered by the STONES, photographed by Tony Gale.

1965

JANUARY
6-8   Irish tour

17   Fly to United States for recording in Los Angeles.

21   Arrive in Sydney for Roy Orbison tour - 3000 fans riot at the airport.

23-30   Australian tour

Release of LP "The Rolling Stones No 2".

FEBRUARY
1-8   New Zealand tour.

10-13   Touring in Australia.

16-17   In Singapore and Hong Kong with the Hollies.

26   Release of "The Last Time"/"Play With Fire".

MARCH
5-18   Major English tour with the Hollies, at Manchester Palace Theatre on March 7 a girl fan fell from the dress circle and was injured.

Thank Your Lucky Stars, July 27th 1964.

MARCH 26-APRIL 2
　　Scandinavian tour and television visit.

APRIL
11　　New Musical Express Poll Winners Concert at Wembley.

17-18　Olympia Theatre, Paris.

22　　Fly to Montreal for Canadian and American tour until May 29.

JUNE
15-18　Short Scottish tour.

24-29　Short Scandinavian visit - in Oslo, Norwegian police with batons knock down rioting fans.

June 26th 1964, the STONES backstage in the ready steady go dressing room. CHARLIE gets in on the Paisley shirt craze 2 years in advance. BRIAN'S striped vest was pinched from his downstairs neighbours, the pretty things.

JULY
29   CHARLIE buys sixteenth century house in Sussex which once belonged to an Archbishop of Canterbury. CHARLIE bought the house from Lord Shawcross, the erstwhile British Attorney-General in the Labour Government.

AUGUST
1   London Palladium.

20   Release of "Satisfaction"/"Spider and the Fly".

23   Security guards hose fans outside Manchester television studios.

AUGUST

24 ROLLING STONES meet Allen Klein for the first time at the Hilton Hotel, London.

28 Andrew Oldham and Allen Klein to con-manage the ROLLING STONES, new contract signed with Decca for five years.

SEPTEMBER

3-5 Ireland

11 German and Austrian tour until September 17.

24 - OCTOBER 17
British tour with Mike Sarne, John Leyton, Spencer Davis. Release of LP "Out of Our Heads".

22 Release of "Get Off of My Cloud"/"The Singer Not The Song".

29 THE STONES fly to Montreal for fourth Canadian/American tour until December 5.

An alternative out-take photo for the first LP.

1966

FEBRUARY
4   Release of "19th Nervous Breakdown"/"As Tears Go By".

13   Ed Sullivan Show in New York.

14   Fly to Sydney for tour which also includes appearances at Brisbane, Adelaide and in New Zealand, St Kilda, Wellington and Auckland on March 1 (St. David's Day).

MARCH
26   European tour until April 5.

APRIL
Release of LP "Aftermath".

MAY
1   New Musical Express Poll Winners Concert at Wembley.

13   Release of "Paint It Black".

JUNE
21   ROLLING STONES sue fourteen hotels over a booking ban in New York for $1,750,850 because the hotels turned down their bookings. They also file a damages suit alleging that the hotels had injured their reputation and claiming that the refusal of bookings amounts to "discrimination on account of national origin" violating New York's civil rights laws.

23   ROLLING STONES arrive in New York for fifth American/Canadian tour, ending on June 28 in Hawaii.

Stones at Ivor Court Jan '65

SEPTEMBER
10 ROLLING STONES appear on Ed Sullivan Show in New York and Ready Steady Go in England.

12 Tour opens in Munster, Germany - fans riot at the opening show.

16 Tom Driberg, MP, to ask a question in the House of Commons to "deplore" the action of a magistrate who called the ROLLING STONES "complete morons" who wore "filthy clothes".

23 Release of "Have You Seen Your Mother Baby"/"Who's Driving Your Plane".

Opening of British tour at London's Albert Hall with reception afterwards. Tour with Ike and Tina Turner and the Yardbirds until October 9.

NOVEMBER
Release of LP "Big Hits High Tide and Green Grass".

DECEMBER
10 New Musical Express rate ROLLING STONES Top British and r & b group, "Satisfaction" as Best Song.

The Stones first major festival appearance at the Richmond Jazz and Blues Festival on 7th August 1964, they received thirty pounds for this performance.

The ever obliging Charlie keeps the fans happy.

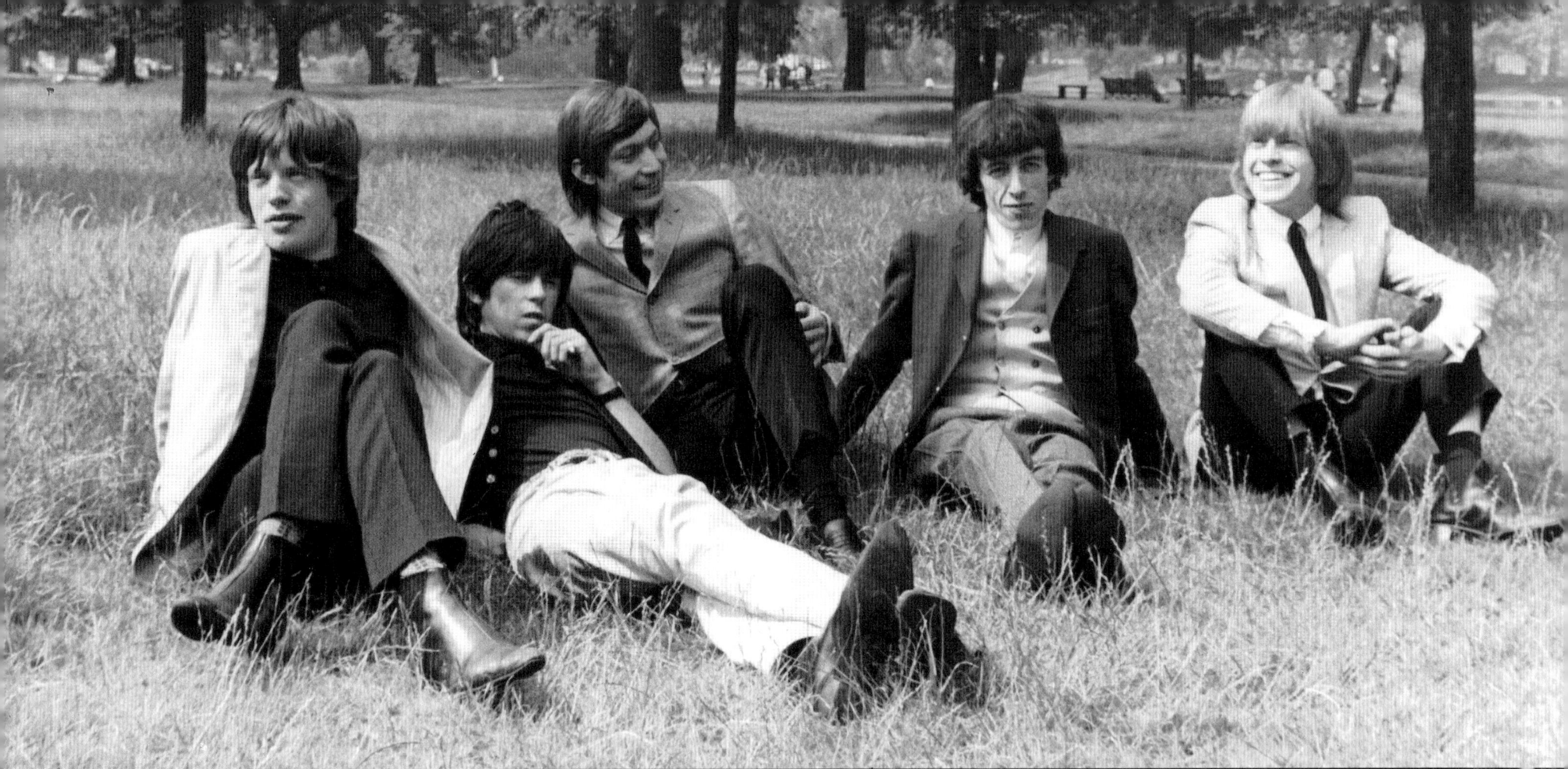
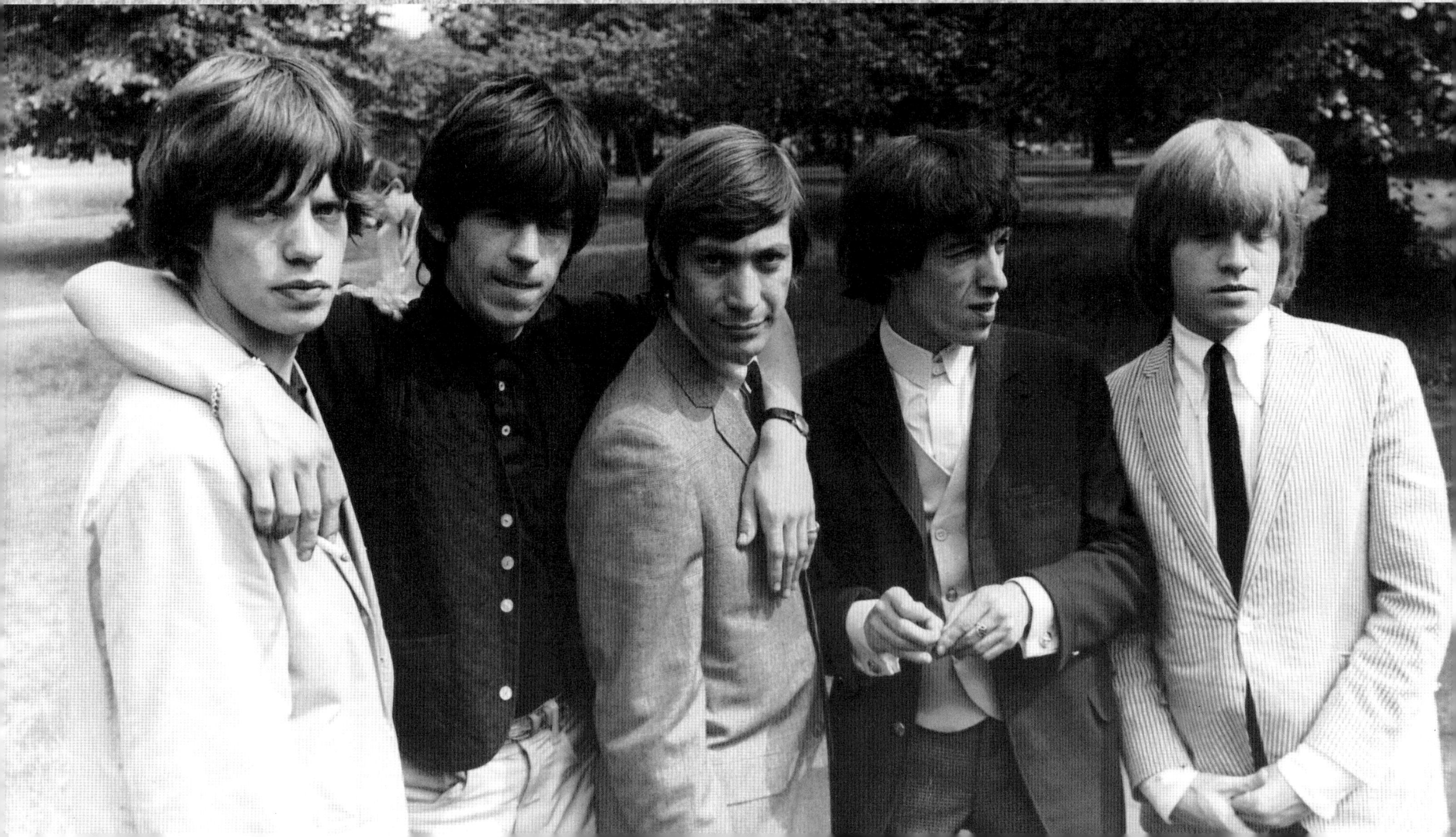

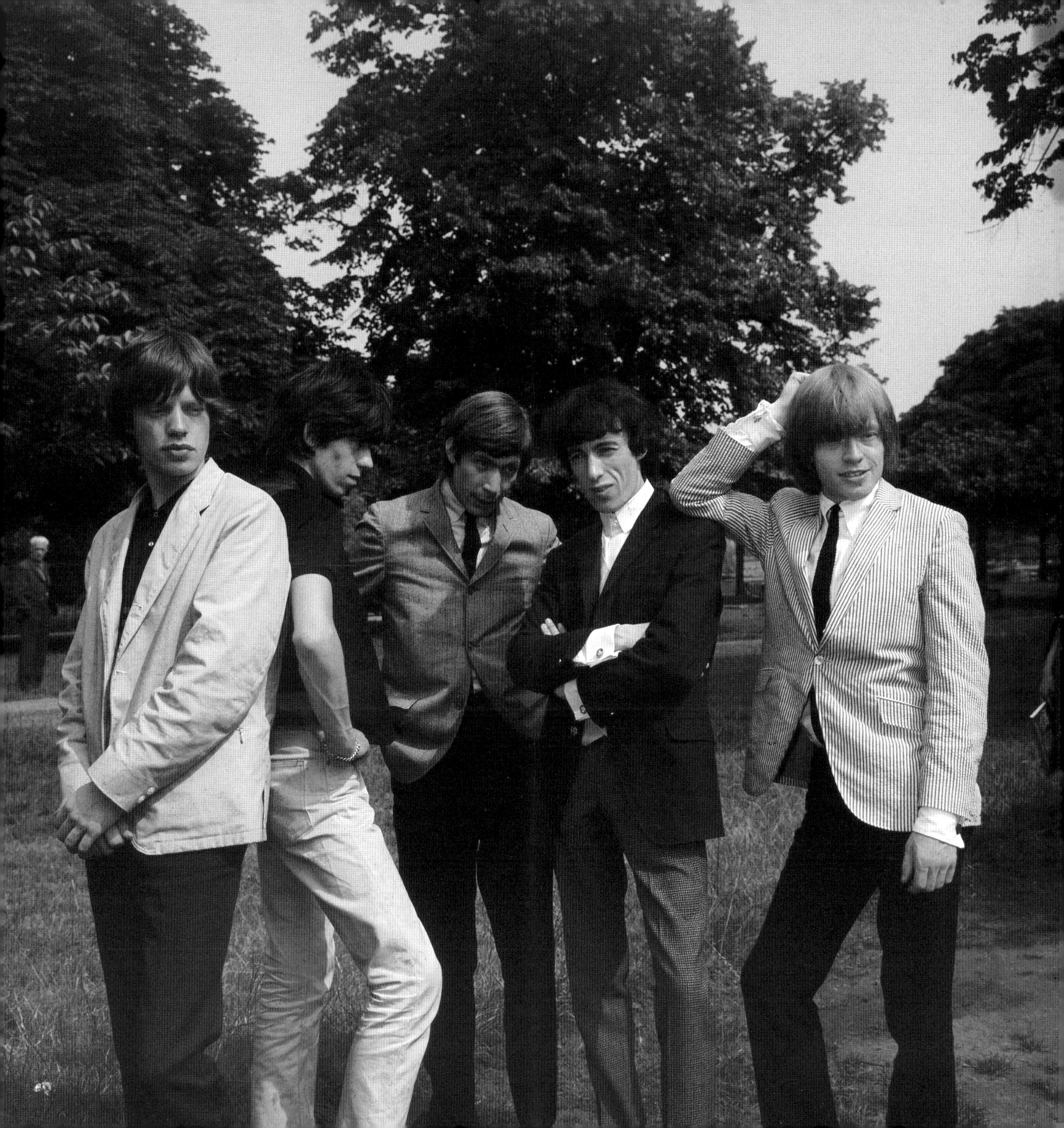

Mick and Keith practice playing Elvis on the piano during a sequence from the film "Charlie is My Darling" recorded in a Belfast hotel room on 4th September 1965.

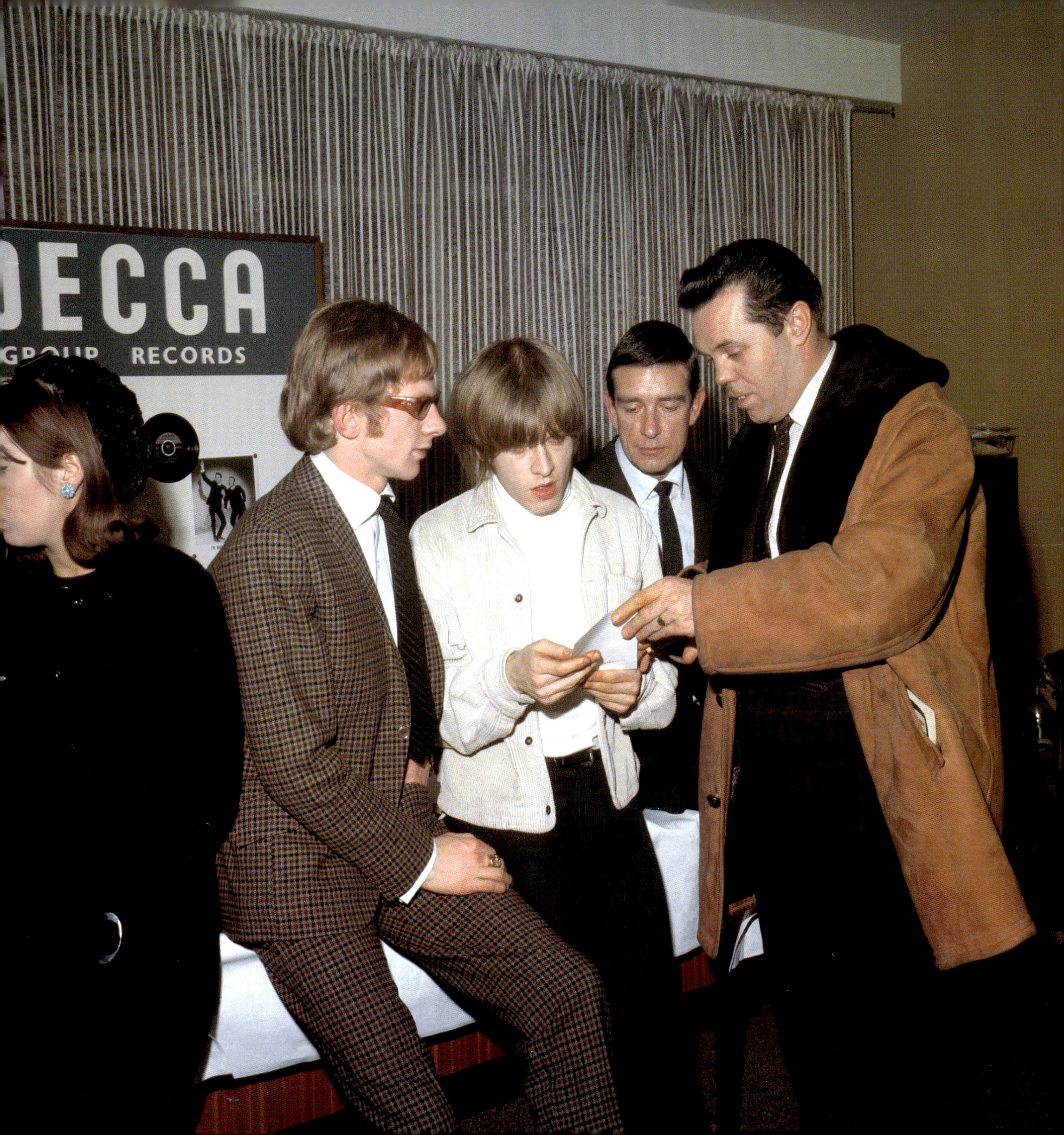
ECCA
RECORDS

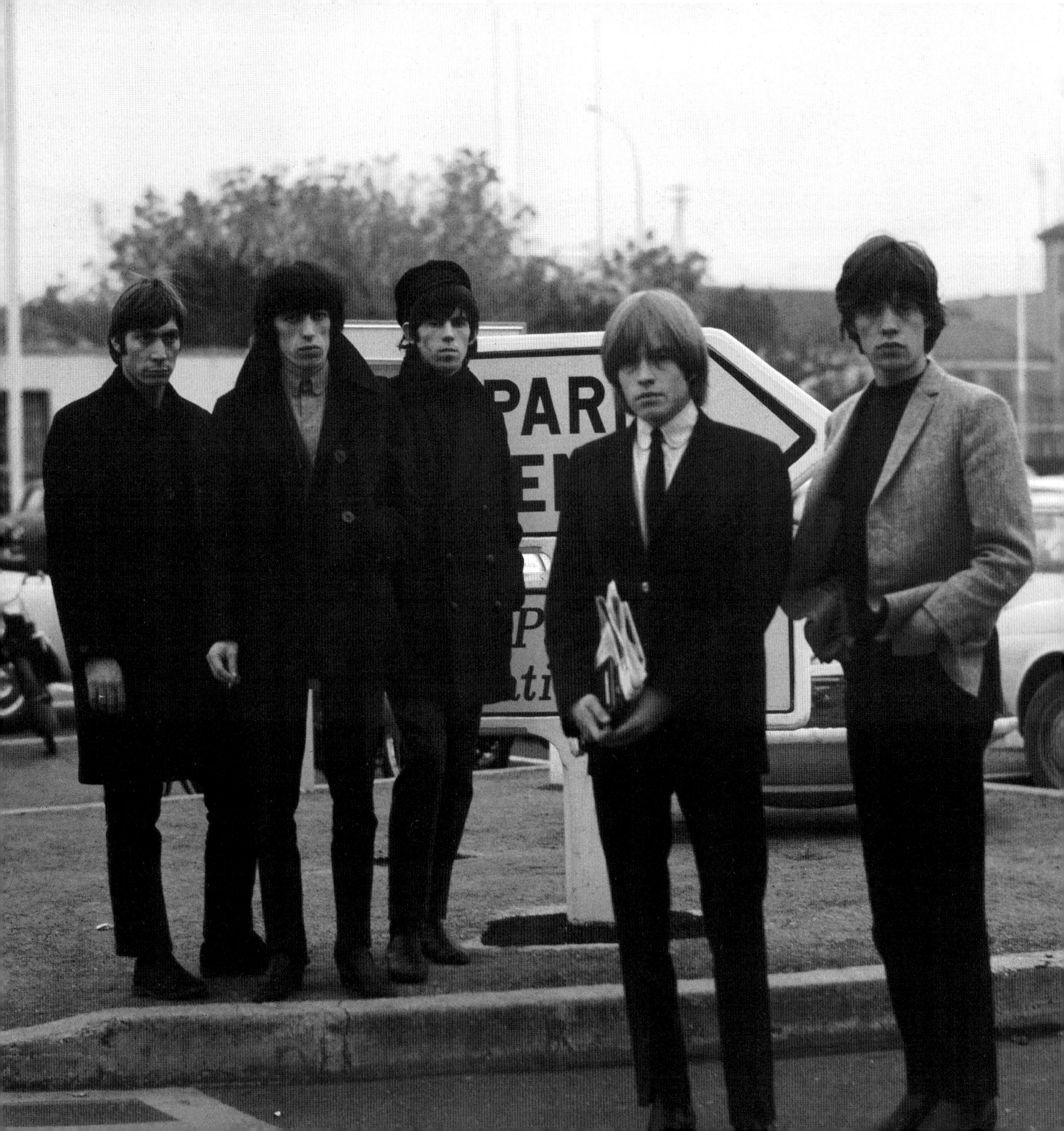

A hand painted poster proudly displays the Stones appearance at the Paris Olympia on 20th October 1964.

N.M.E's tip for the top - The Rockin' Berries.

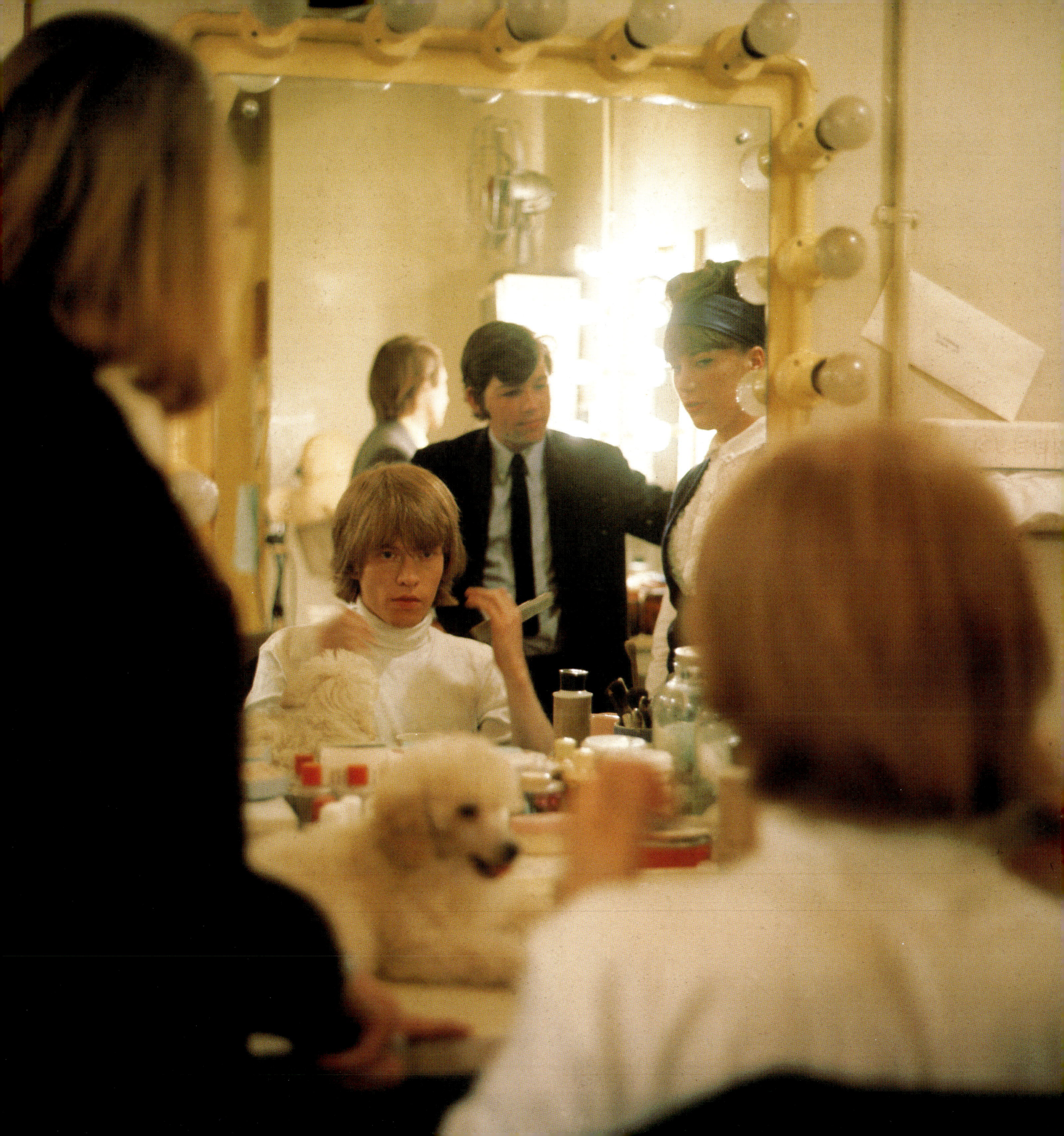

"Cup O' tea guv!"

27/5/66 Playing Dulcimer on "I am Waiting" Ready Steady Go.

Brian playing a different raga style on the Indiana Sita for Paint it Black broadcast on Ready Steady Go 27/5/66.

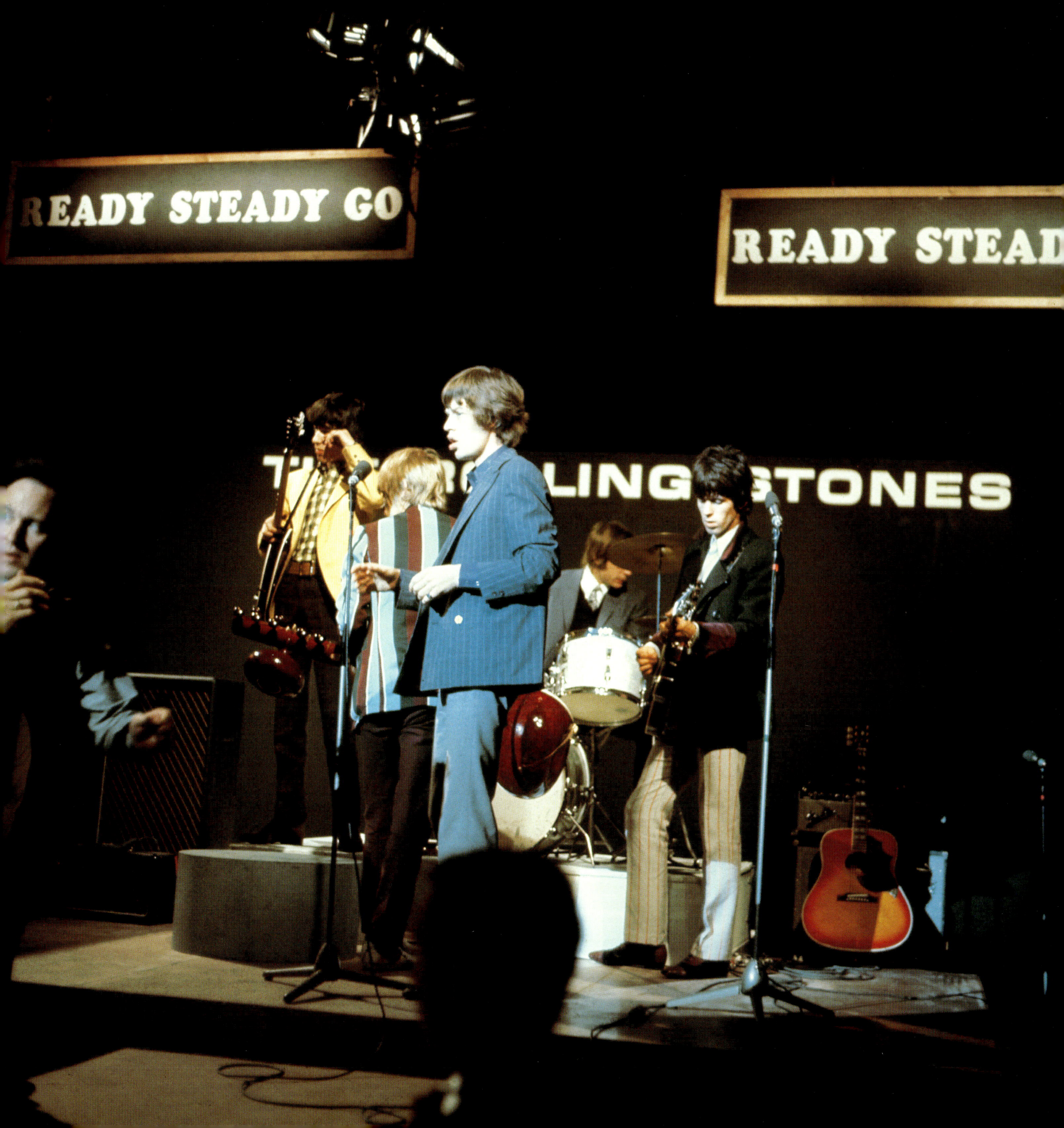
READY STEADY GO
READY STEAD
THE ROLLING STONES

Brian upset at an article while the polo neck sweatered Mick Jagger doesn't seem to think it all bad.

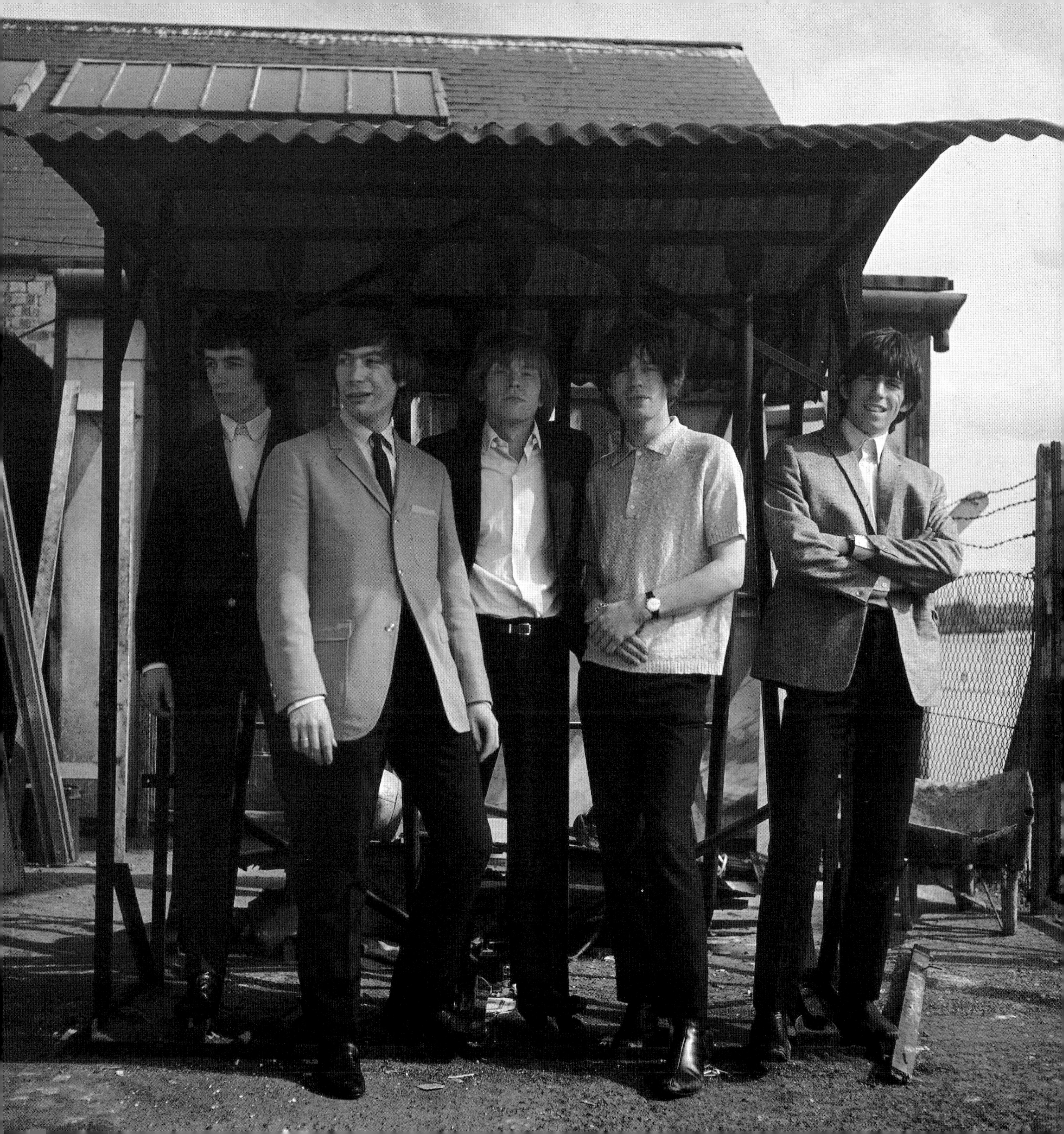

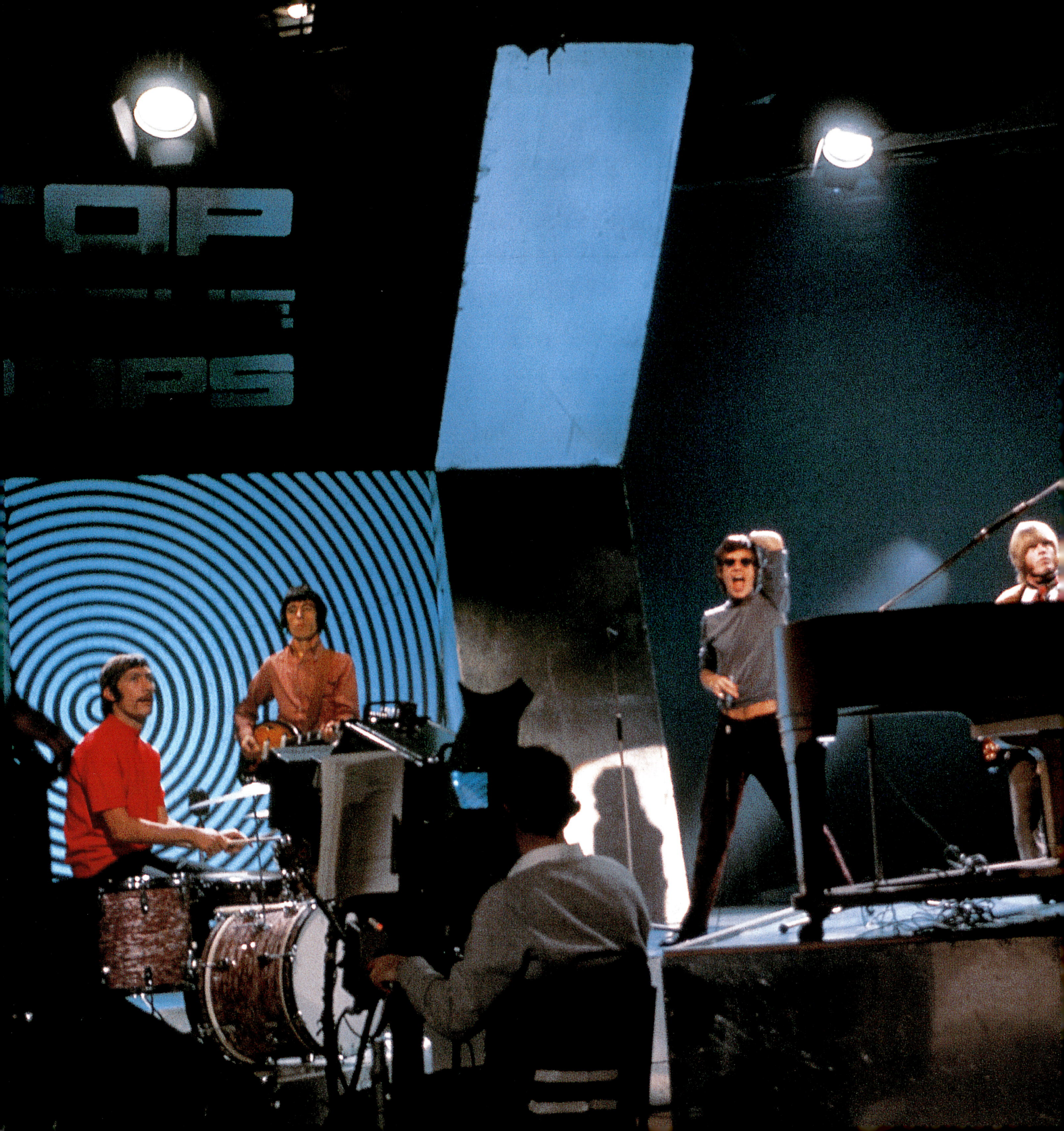

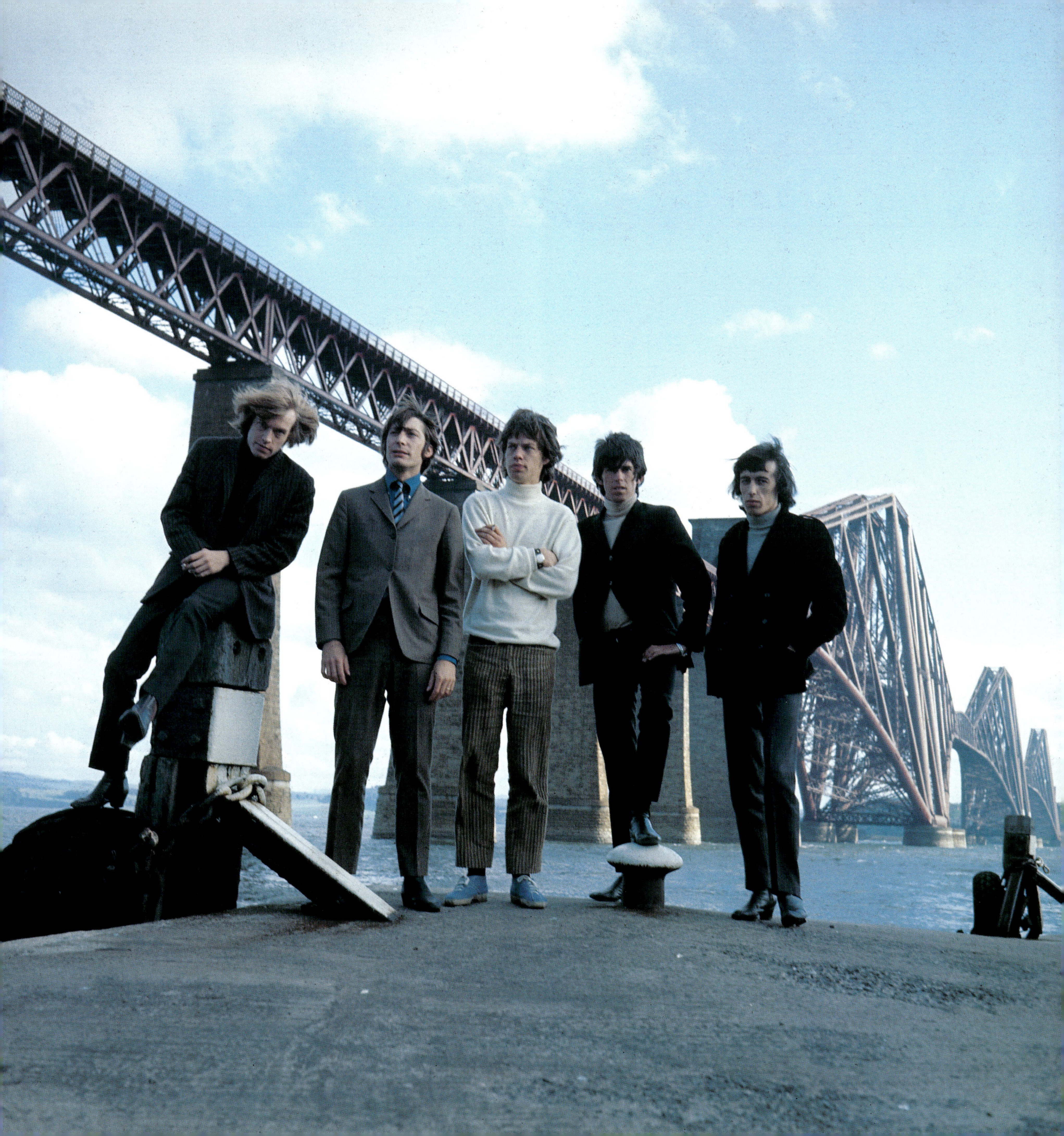

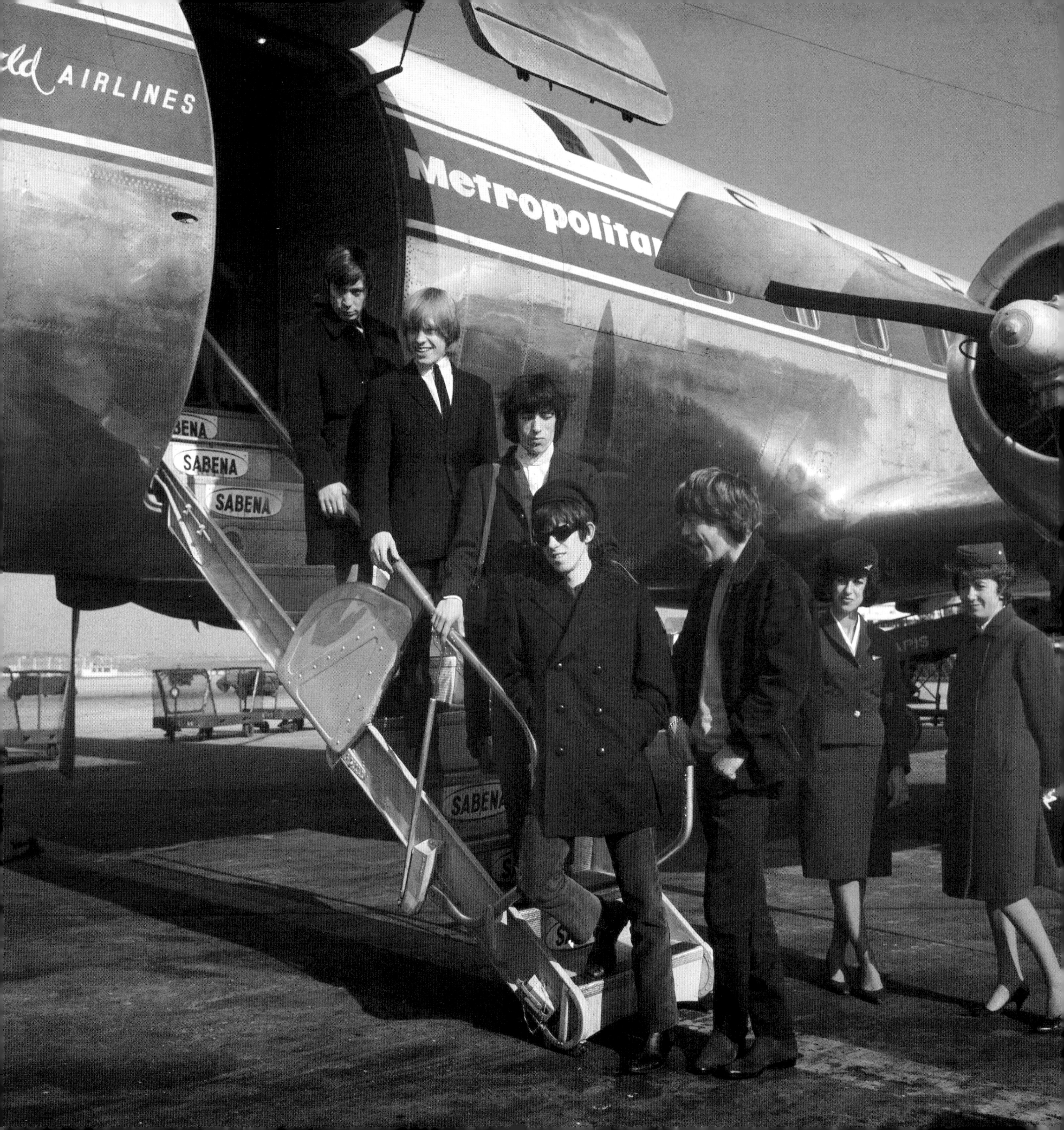
AIRLINES
Metropolitan
SABENA
SABENA
SABENA
SABENA

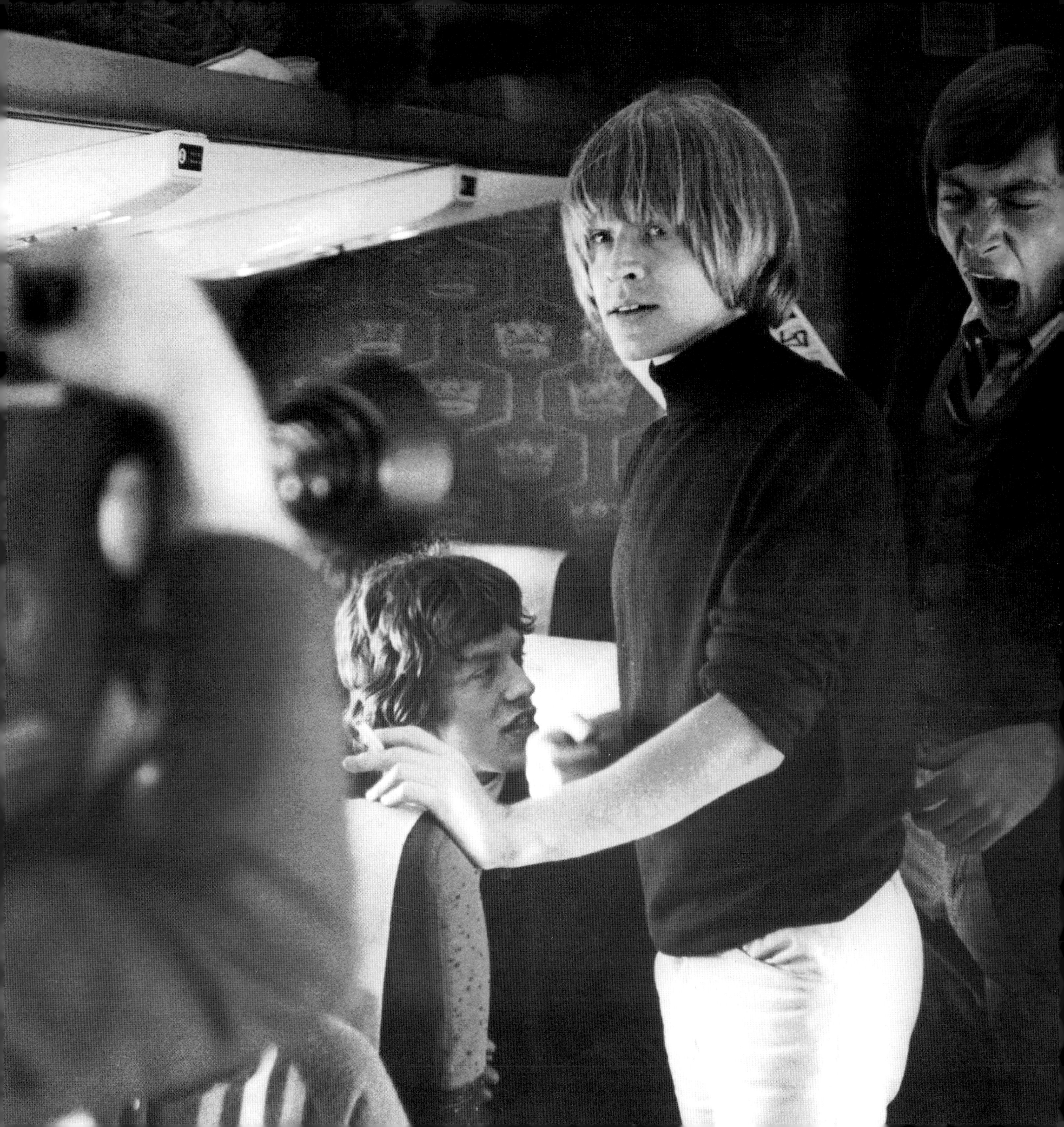

The Green Park (opposite the Hard Rock Cafe, London) photo call in January 1967

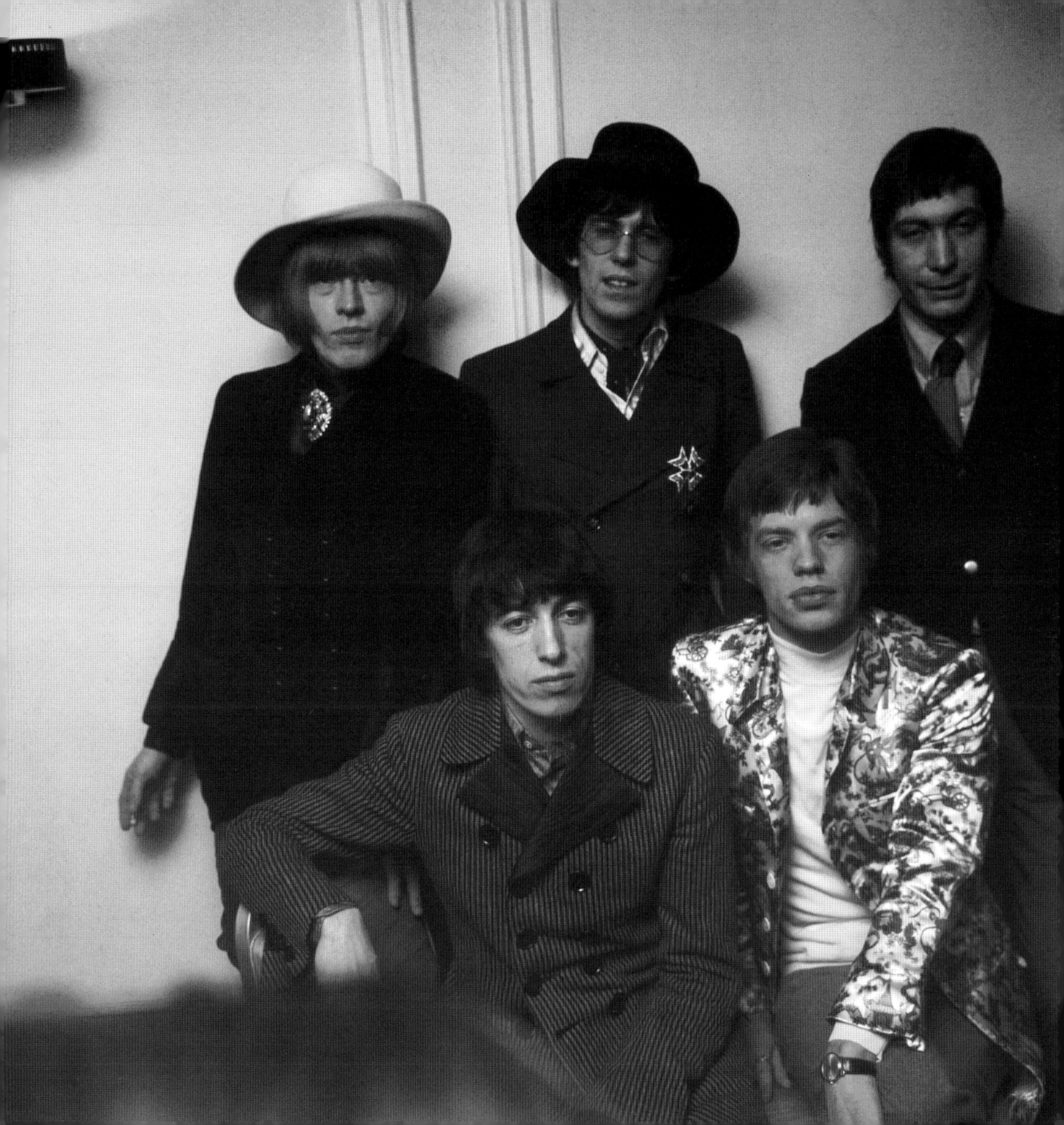

The band rehearse for the Eamonn Andrew's Show on 5th February 1967.

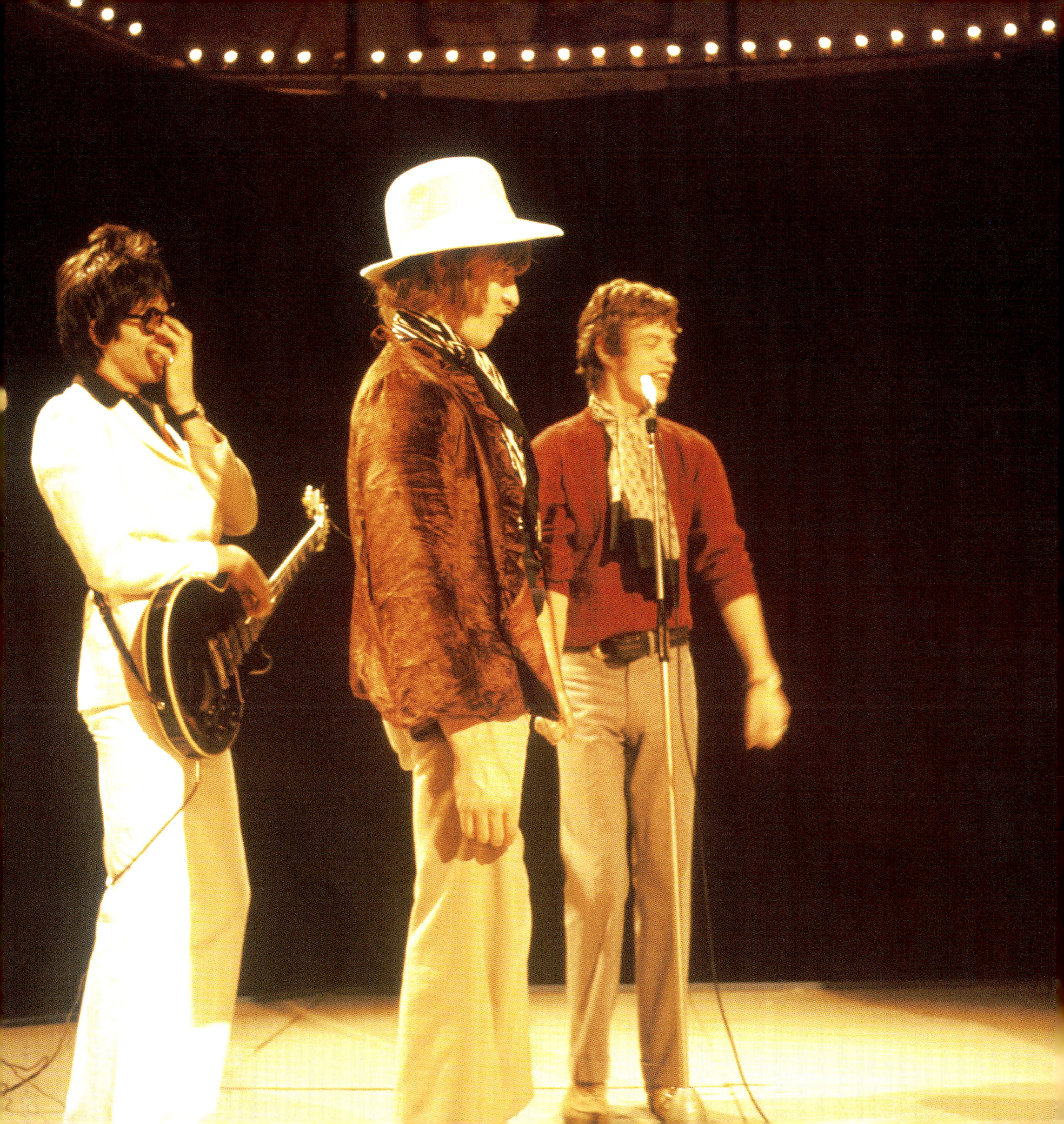

1967

JANUARY
13   New York, Ed Sullivan Show.

20   Release of "Between The Buttons" LP, in America.

22   London Palladium - the ROLLING STONES cause sensation refusing to go on the revolving stage on ITV's top show.

28   Release of "Let's Spend The Night Together"/"Ruby Tuesday".

FEBRUARY
2   London, on recorded Top of The Pops.

MARCH
25   Opening of European tour at Oerbro, Sweden, until April 17.

APRIL
8   Milan, Pallazzo des Sportes .... Daily Express publishes remarks made by Olympic Gold Medallist Lynn Davies concerning the alleged behaviour of the ROLLING STONES in a German hotel. MICK JAGGER replies from Rome that "the accusations are disgusting and completely untrue. We deny that we were badly behaved. I cannot remember when we have behaved better. We hardly used the public rooms in this hotel. They were crammed with athletes behaving very badly".

Brian backstage at Monterey Pop Festival, California, the only representative from the Stones for the first of the great festivals of the sixties.

APRIL
13 ROLLING STONES' first visit behind the Iron Curtain - Warsaw. The Warsaw police use batons and tear-gas to break up crowd of 3000 teenagers trying to storm the Palace of Culture where the concert was held. Riot scenes outside.

MAY
12 New Musical Express Poll Winners Concert at Wembley.

AUGUST
18 Release of "We Love You"/"Dandelion" - described as a thank-you to fans who were loyal during the trials etc.

26 MICK JAGGER and Marianne Faithful with the Beatles to see the Maharishi - during this weekend Brian Epstein died.

SEPTEMBER
At the end of this month the ROLLING STONES announce that they have broken away from Andrew Oldham and will in future produce their own records.

DECEMBER
Release of LP "Their Satanic Majesties".

A rare colour photo of Brian at the Monterey Pop Festival. He introduced Jimi Hendrix's memorable performance on June 18th 1967.

"We Love You"

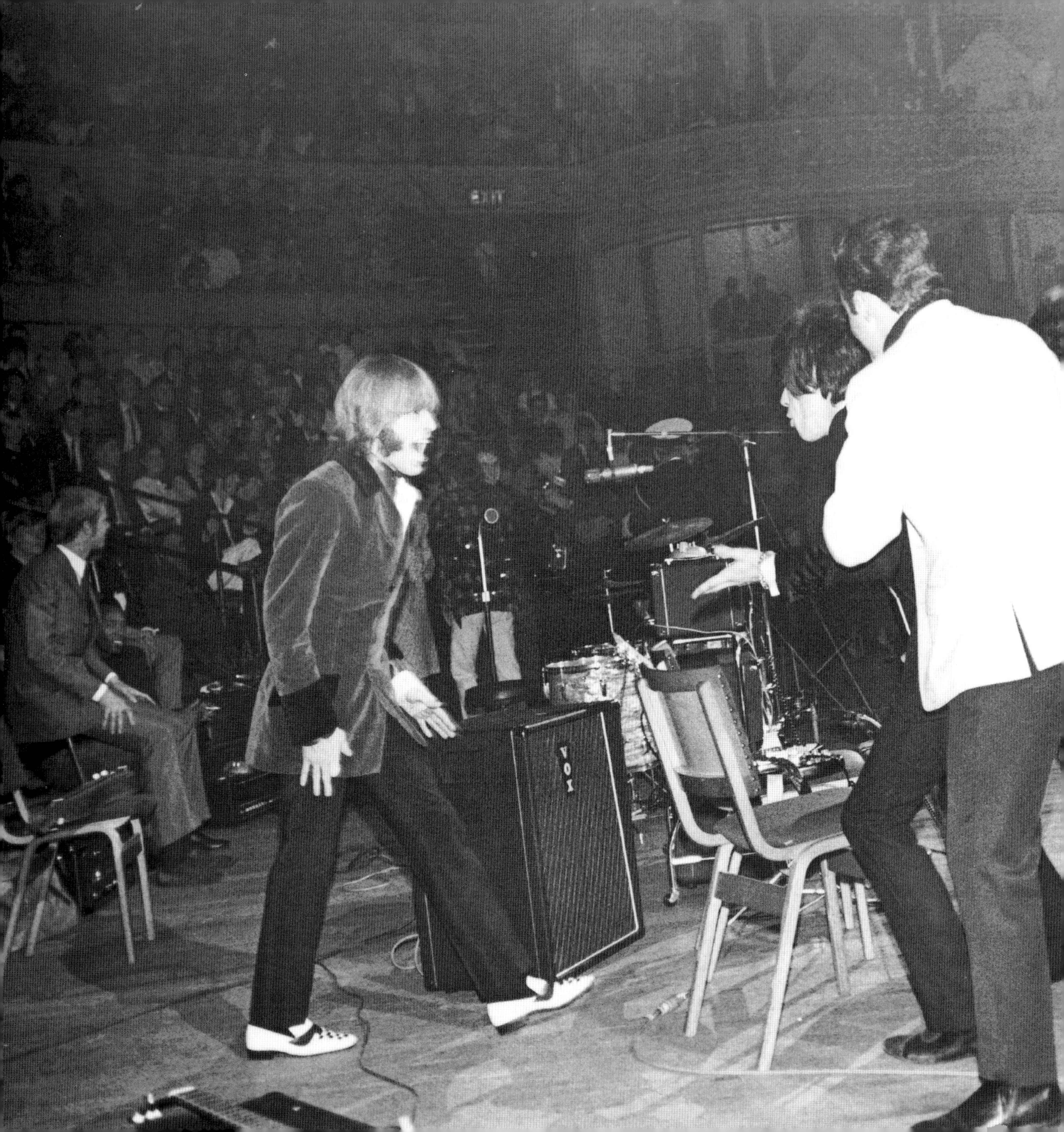
EXIT
VOX

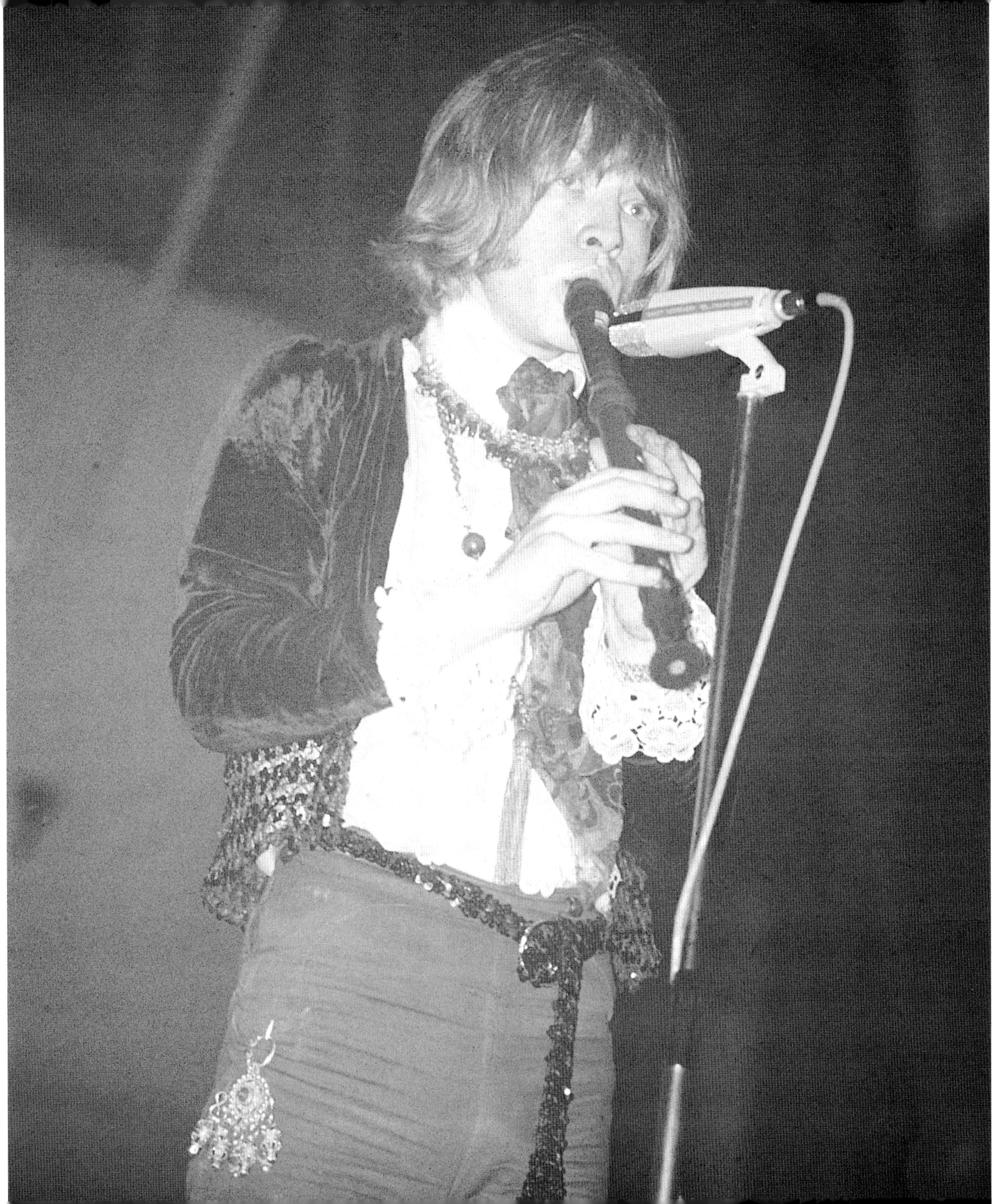

Brian and Mick at the Supremes party in January 1968.

1968

JANUARY
4   Daily Sketch report that the University of California in Los Angeles is insisting that students taking music degrees must study the ROLLING STONES' music as the music professor feels they have made an important contribution to modern music.

MARCH
18   Serafina Watts born to CHARLIE and Shirley.

MAY
12   New Musical Express Poll Winners Concert Wembley.
25   Release of "Jumpin' Jack Flash"/"Child of the Moon".
31   Announcement of ROLLING STONES making a film with Jean-Luc Godard, "One to One".
During the autumn MICK JAGGER started work on the film "Performance" with James Fox.

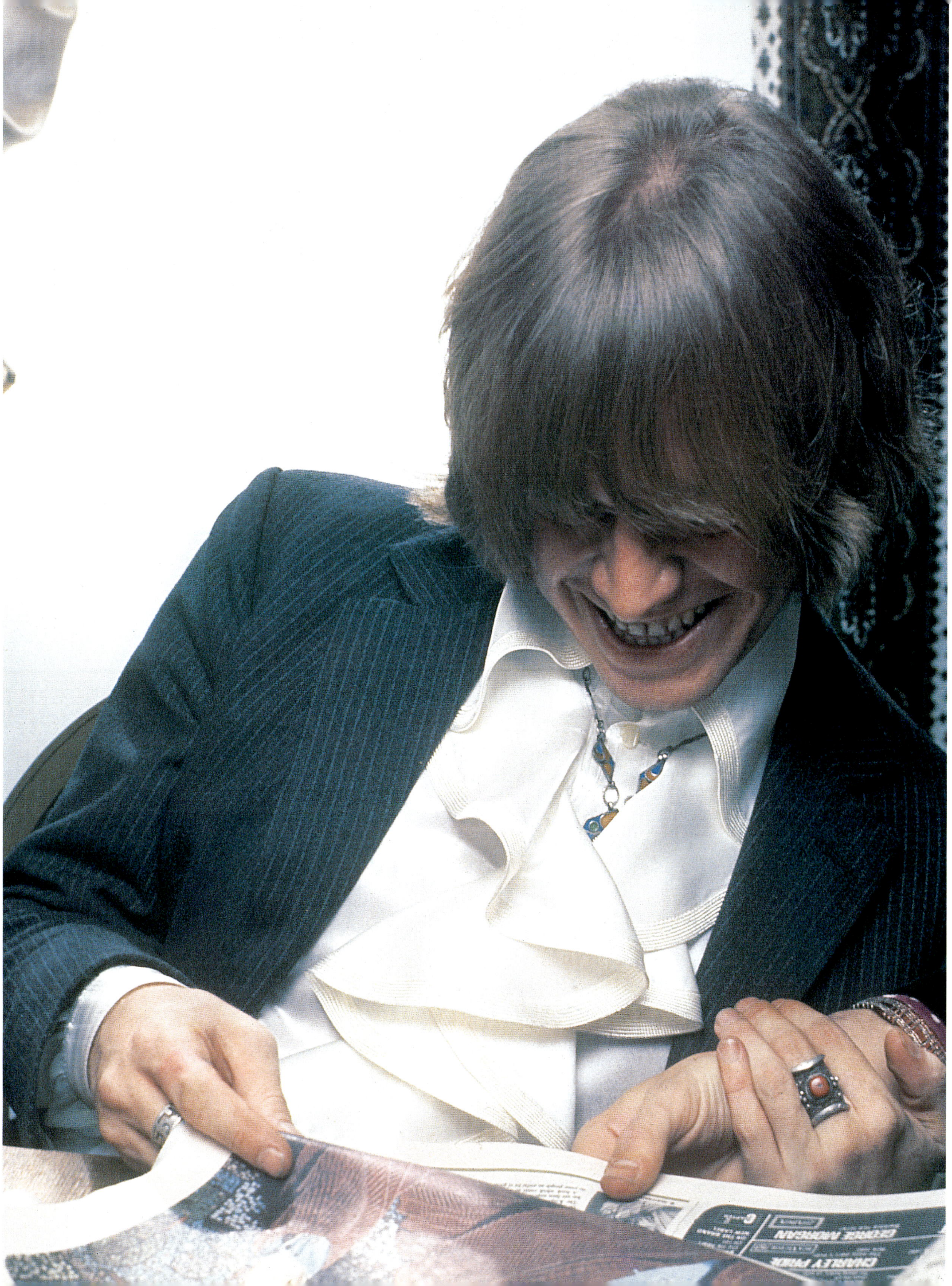
GEORGE MORGAN
CHARLEY PRIDE

Brian - The perfect looking stone 1965.

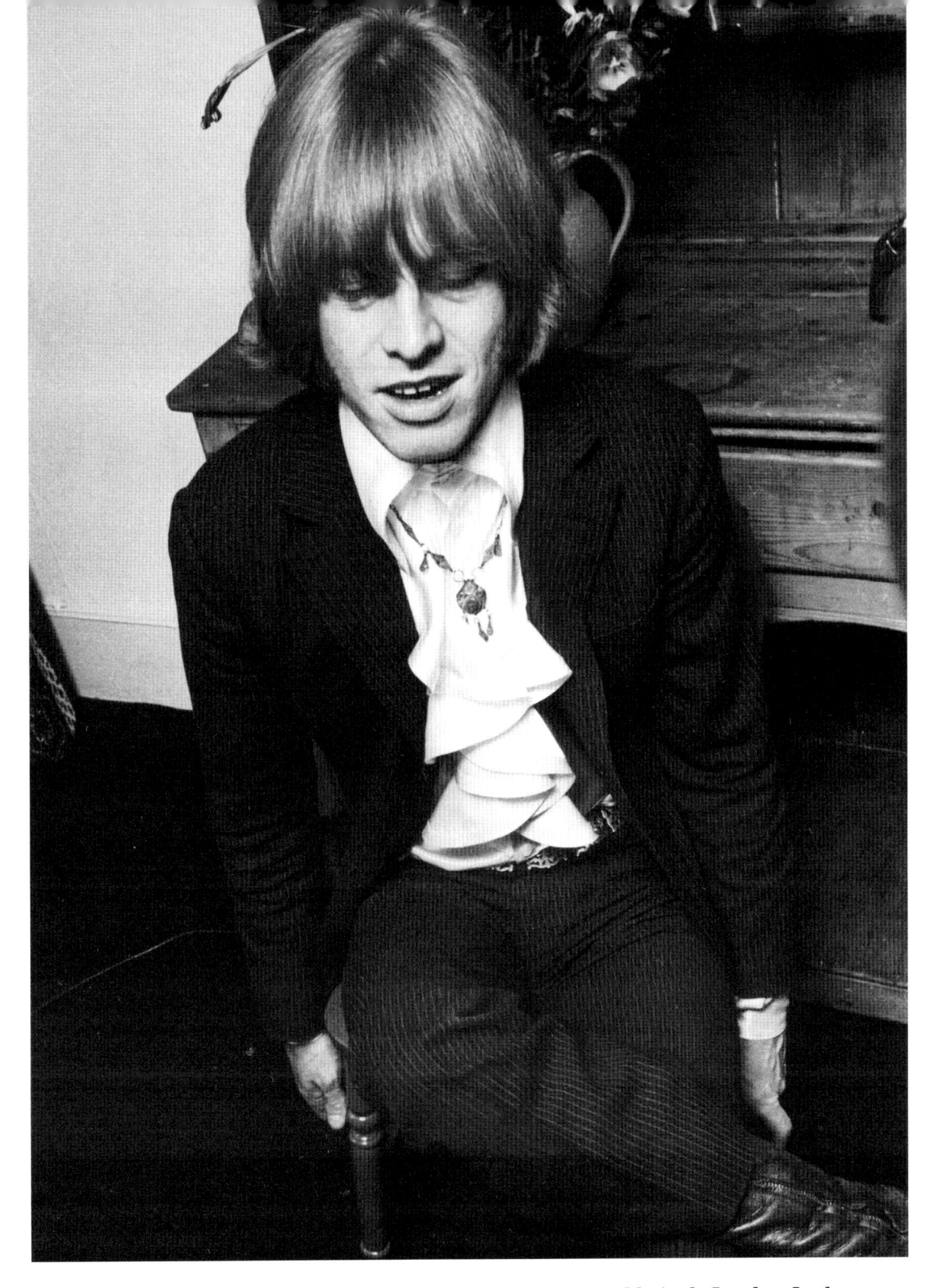

May 1968 Brian poses for a publicity shot for "Jumpin' Jack Flash" at the Cumberland Hotel Marble Arch, London. In the same month Brian was victim to a second suspicious drugs bust.

SEPTEMBER

4 ROLLING STONES latest single in America "Street Fighting Man" being banned by some American radio stations because it might incite riots, etc.

6 London, MICK JAGGER appears on the David Frost television show.

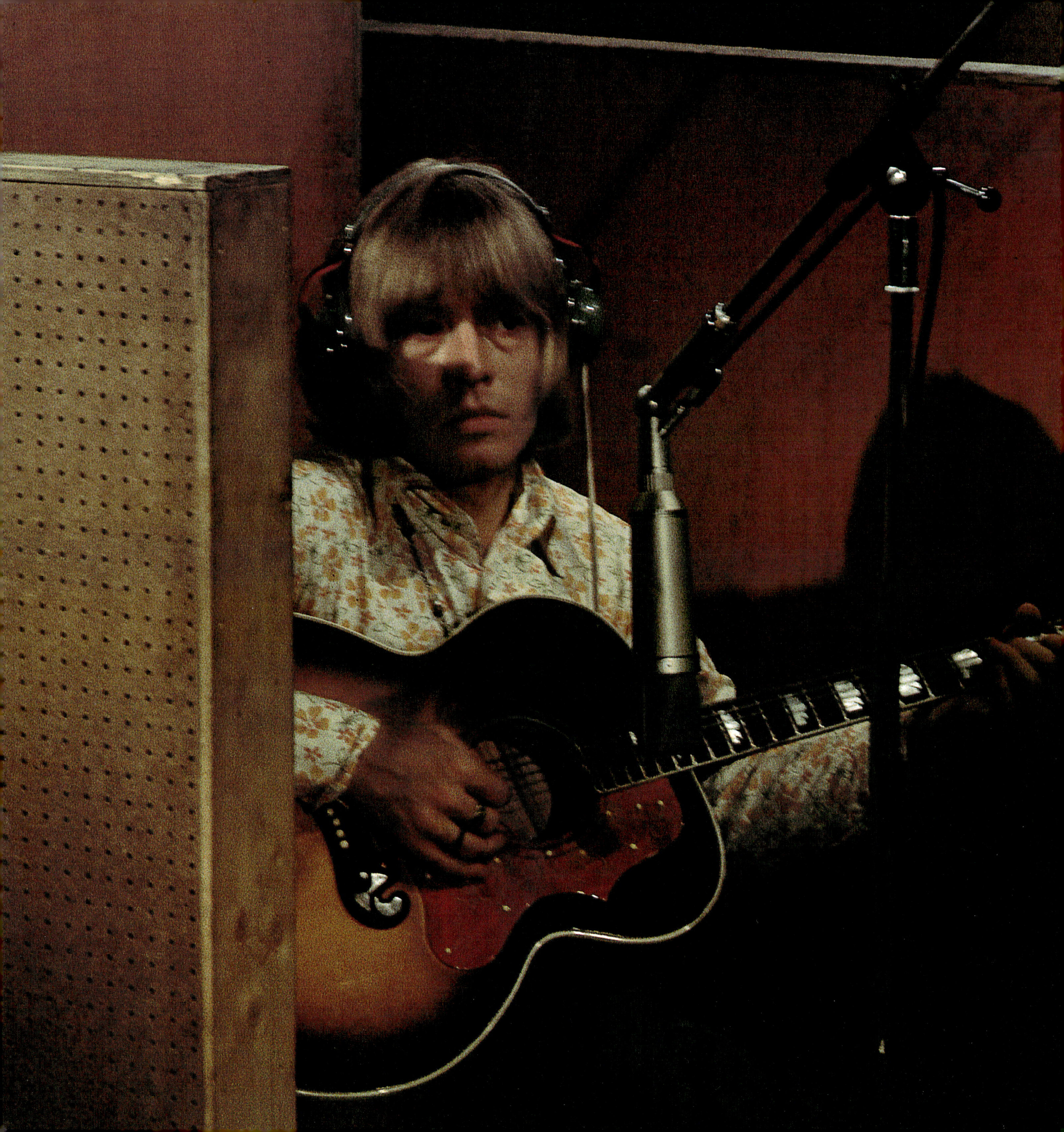

The ideal English couple, Marianne Faithful symbolising the Sixties English look.

Brian and model Donyale Luna at "Rock 'n' Roll Circus Show" being made for television at Stonebridge House, Wembley.

NOVEMBER

21 BRIAN JONES buys A A Milne's old home, (where he wrote the Winnie the Pooh books) Cotchford Farm, in Sussex.

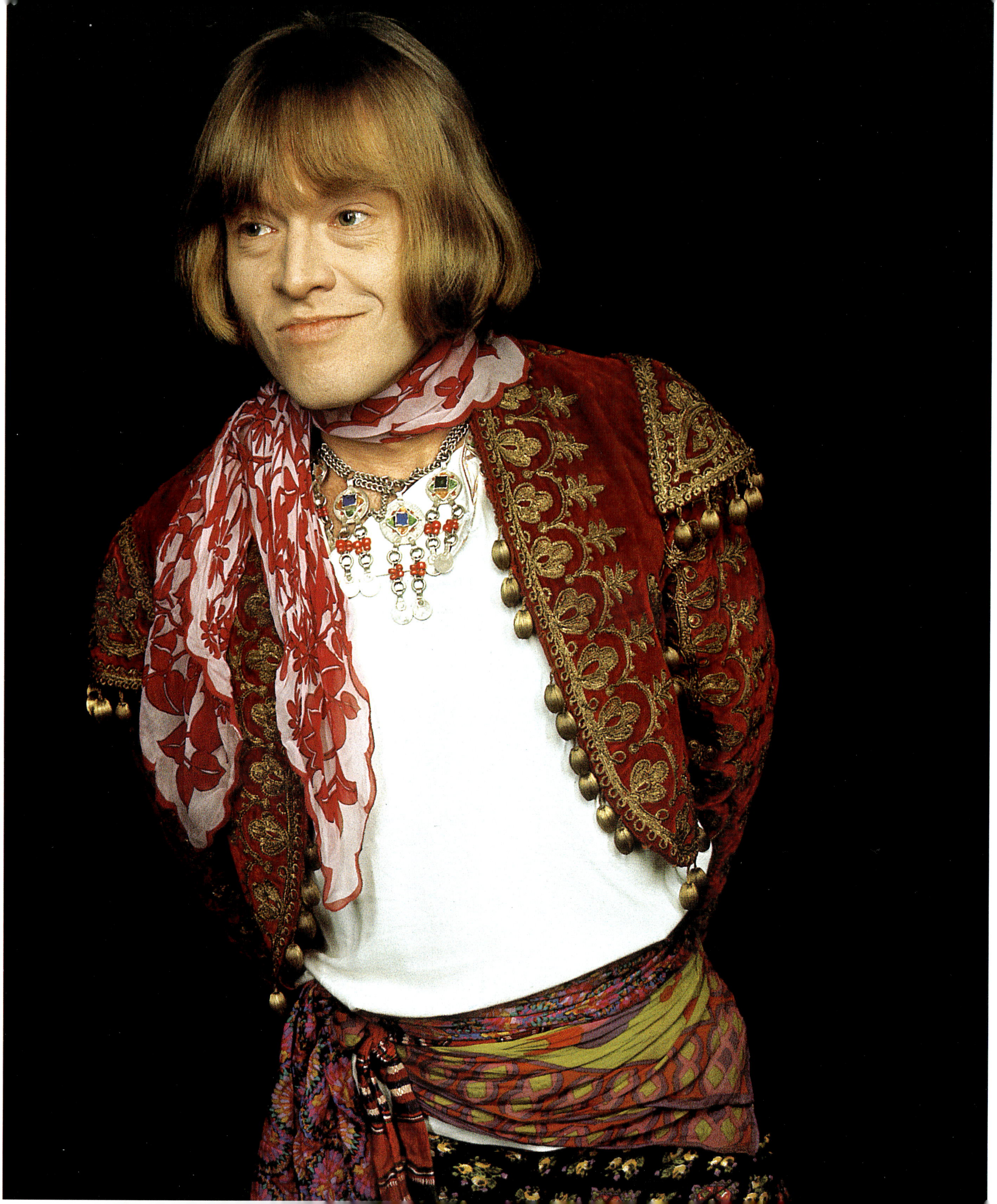

With Brian's Spanish outfits off, The Stones develop that stoned expression.

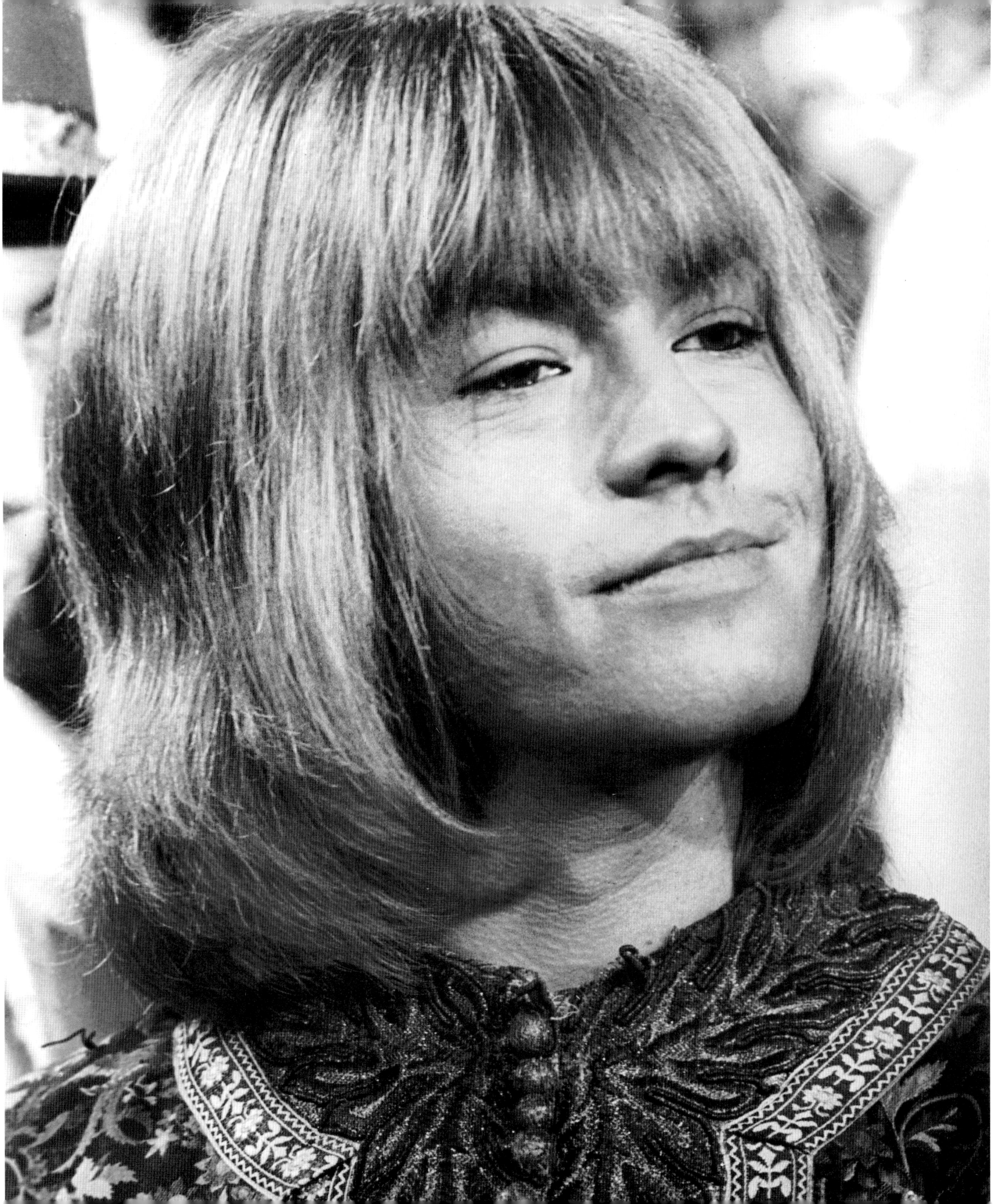

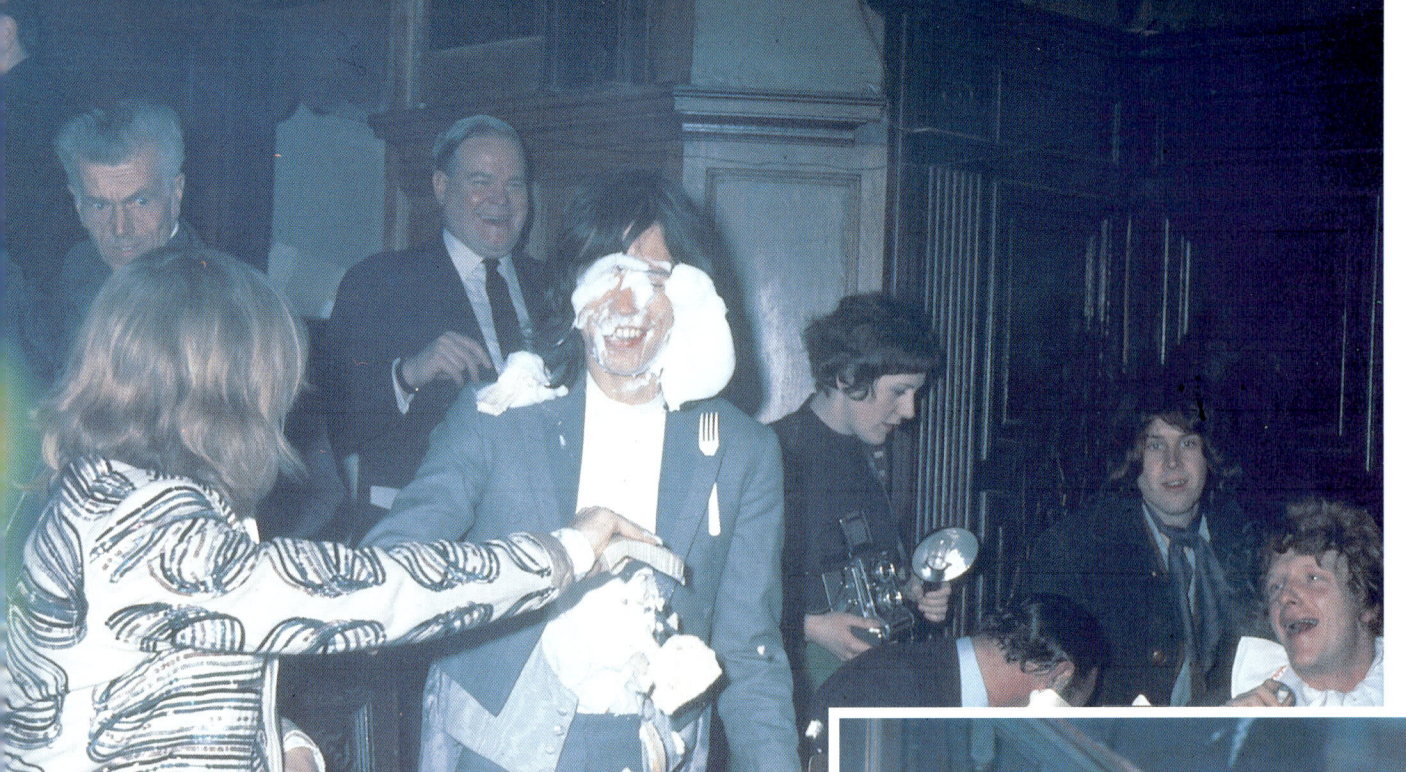

Les Perrin the Rolling Stones P.R. man gets his own back.

DECEMBER

5 ROLLING STONES hold a 'beggars banquet' at Elizabethan rooms in London to mark release of their LP "Beggars Banquet". Lord Harlech deputises for KEITH RICHARD who is ill. They surprise guests with a custard pie throwing party.

12 ROLLING STONES "Rock 'n' Roll Circus" filmed at Wembley studios for television - friends include John and Yoko Lennon.

18 MICK AND Marianne, KEITH and Anita, leave for Brazil on holiday.

Release of LP "Beggars' Banquet".

The Stones last official photograph with Brian at Rehearsals for the Frost on Sunday Show at Stonebridge House, Wembley, London, on the 4th December 1968 screened on the 8th December 1968. The Stones performed Street Fighting Man (banned in the U.S. for its inflammatory Nature).

1969

JANUARY
17 MICK and KEITH asked to leave the Hotel Crillon in Lima because they were wearing pop art trousers and nothing else. They move to the exclusive Hotel Belivar.

MAY
28 Announcement made that MICK JAGGER will be playing "Ned Kelly" in the forthcoming film.

JUNE
8 BRIAN JONES leaves the ROLLING STONES. MICK TAYLOR to replace him.
13 A photocall held in Hyde Park to introduce MICK TAYLOR.

JULY
3 BRIAN JONES dies at his home near Hartfield (Cotchford Farm).